What others are saying . . .

trish ♡ SO-BND-501

476-2896

march '99

"All the world is a stage—also the inner world. If we fully assimilate this metaphor, we will know ourselves better, we will be empowered, and we will be able to play. Vivian King's book is a great and thorough guide to our inner theatre and the immense possibilities it holds within."

PIERO FERRUCCI, PH.D.
Author, *What We May Be*

". . . an exceptionally creative and practical book, providing readers with significant personal and transpersonal growth opportunities. Fun-loving. *Play* is a key word in Vivian's work."

JOHN CULLEN, PH.D.
President, International Association for
Managerial and Organizational Psychosynthesis

". . . original. Authentic. Novel. Most progressive."

JANIS MIKHAILOVS
Rector, International Institute of
Practical Psychology, Riga, Latvia

"The methodology Vivian has developed crosses barriers between therapy and business, between men and women, and even between countries and cultures. It is a diamond among gems."

ROGER MOORE
Project Manager, Aerospace Industry

"Wonderful! Creative! Enlightened! *Soul Play* is a delightful sourcebook for all artists, particularly theatre artists. Bravo!"

JEAN SABATINE
Professor, Drama Dept., University of Connecticut
Author, *Movement Training for the Stage and Screen*

"*Soul Play* is a pleasure to read and absorb. The author's own joy and enthusiasm positively shine through this book. With beautiful logic and detail, Vivian King emphasizes the importance of the synthesis of all the parts of the psyche. . . . An extremely user-friendly book that will be a very useful addition to the list of core Psychosynthesis resources for students and trainers alike."

GUY PETTITT, M.D.
Whole Life Endeavors, New Zealand

Soul Play

Soul Play

Turning Your Daily Dramas into Divine Comedies

Vivian King, Ph.D.

ANT HILL PRESS
Georgetown, Massachusetts

Copyright © 1998
Vivian King, Ph.D.

ISBN # 0-9655067-1-1

First Printing 1998

Ant Hill Press
P.O. Box 10
Georgetown, MA 01833
(978) 352-9976 • Fax (978) 352-5586
http://www.ReadersNdex.com/northstar

Cover design: Salwen Studios, Keene, NH

Cover montage by Hans Christian Andersen. The original screen belongs to the
Hans Christian Andersen Museum, Odense, Denmark. Used with permission.
Back cover photo: Kim Jew, Albuquerque, NM
Editor: John Niendorff
Printed in the United States of America

The author gratefully acknowledges the following individuals and publishers for granting permission to use their materials:
"For Those Who Possess Their Own Theater Within," *Satan Sleeps with the Holy: Word Paintings* by Carolyn Mary Kleefeld. © 1986 Horse and Bird Press, Los Angeles. Reprinted with permission of the author.
"And More," by E. B. de Vito. © 1992. Printed in *Christian Science Monitor*. Reprinted with permisson of the author.
Excerpt from "The Man Who Wasn't Afraid," © 1994 Wild Woman Enterprises, Albuquerque, NM.
Quotes from *Book of Qualities*, J. Ruth Gendler, © 1988, HarperCollins Publishers.
Excerpt from *Dancing with Our Dreams,* Victoria Gamber, © 1992, unpublished manuscript. Scottsdale, AZ..

Inner Theatre™ is a trademark of Vivian King, Ph.D.

Publisher's Cataloging-in-Publication
King, Vivian.
      Soul play : turning your daily dramas into divine comedies
/ Vivian King. — 1st ed.
      p. cm.
      Includes bibliographical references and index.
      ISBN: 0-9655067-1-1

      1. Will. 2. Psychosynthesis. 3. Psychology, Applied.
I. Title

BF611.K56 1998   158.9
                           QBI98-288

This book is dedicated to . . .

my beloved son, Mark Adams –
actor, musician, and scientist.

It is . . .

For those who possess their own theater within,
Who reserve the loge seats for themselves,
Having available whatever they care to nibble on . . .

To go to most of society's entertainment
Is an unnecessary distance to travel
And usually less interesting
Than their own dramas within

– CAROLYN MARY KLEEFELD, in *Satan Sleeps with the Holy*

Acknowledging . . .

Allen and Fannie King—for setting a beautiful stage for my play on Earth and for recognizing my soul from the very beginning.

Roberto Assagioli, Robert Gerard, Piero Ferrucci, and many Psychosynthesis colleagues—for developing and refining principles for personal, transpersonal, and social synthesis.

My many students and clients—for sharing their experiences with the theatre metaphor, thereby encouraging me to continue developing this innovative approach to change. Special thanks to those whose stories I have included in this text.

Cait Wellsinger, Trudy Dunfee, Patricia Cox, Madelaine Weiner, Mirial Buller, Marilyn Barry, Deborah Onken, Fran Pieper, Carolyn Heggen, Carolyn Johns, and Vonda Long—for being loving and faithful members of my supporting cast.

Robert Reiher—for inspiring, encouraging, and believing in me.

Greg and Ruth Whitten—for technological support and for making my life easier.

John Niendorff—for being diplomatic, sensitive, and skillful in editing this book. And for maintaining a good sense of humor.

Ralph Melcher—for preliminary editing, and Virginia MacIvor Meyn for proofreading.

Nancy Salwen—for perception, persistence, and patience in designing the cover of the book.

George Trim—for seeing the value of my work and being willing to publish and distribute this book to the world's actors.

Program

Previewing

the

Production

Opening the Door

Welcome to the Inner Theatre. The door is open. Come in and take a seat while I introduce you to *Soul Play.* Please sit back, relax, and enjoy this preview.

As the author, I have the pleasure of introducing you to an *entertaining* way to turn your daily dramas into magical moments. I encourage you to let go of the myth that change comes *only* through suffering. Suffering is often a catalyst for change, of course, but *you don't have to suffer to change*! The old saying "No pain, no gain" is a myth that has served us in the past, but there is another way. That way is to change through inspiration, conscious choice, and for the simple joy of it. As theologian Thomas Aquinas said in the thirteenth century, "You change people by delight, you change people by pleasure." This book is about taking charge of your life and doing it with delight and pleasure.

Having said that, I'd like to acknowledge the fact that contemporary life isn't easy, and often it's far from humorous. From our everyday perspective, life seems complex and chaotic. Often we look around with an air of masked indifference to see if others are having fun yet. We wonder how, or if, they are making sense of the madness. The accompanying question is: are we, ourselves, making sense of it?

Newspapers, television, radio, and computer hotlines thrive on the trauma of drama. To accommodate our curiosity, the media captures the colorful pageant of other people's lives and reflects it back to us bigger than life. It keeps us in suspense by reporting tangled webs of relationships and business deals. And since we have some version of the same tangled webs in our own lives, we become a captive audience.

Most of us are mesmerized by the soap operas and scandals of public personalities, be they performers, preachers, or politicians. We tune in to find out what the latest scuttlebutt is all about: Did the politician seduce the secretary? Was perjury committed? Who leaked the information? Who's masterminding the dirt-dig? What are the consequences?

We're curious to know: Is the famous athlete really a killer? Will there be justice in the courtroom? Which set of lawyers will pull off the cleverest performance? What will happen to the children of the murdered mother?

We stay tuned: Is the heroine sleeping with the enemy? Will her husband find out? Who's the real father of the baby? Is the mayor on cocaine? Will the preacher go to jail for misappropriating parish funds? And, who *really* is responsible for the death of the Queen of Hearts?

We become part of the feeding frenzy as the person in the spotlight is scrutinized to the nth degree and every angle of the situation is reported, discussed, debated, critiqued, and judged. Opinions are drawn. Sides are taken. The conflict rages. Eventually the production ends in pain and tragedy, or in resolution and redemption. As in every theatre drama, life's narratives open, unfold, and eventually fade from public consciousness.

In the noisy display of news and entertainment, we recognize our own sick and savage stories, as well as our sane and sacred ones. At least we know we're not alone in the confusion. But this doesn't necessarily mean the confusion is any more bearable.

Invariably, every light casts a shadow; every action leads to a reaction. There is something about human nature that militates against monotony; something that defies one-tone, one-purpose, one-theme.

Captivating entertainment is based on contrast or conflict. Suspense is built when that which pulls us forward clashes with that which holds us back. Either we become mired in the controversy and continue to suffer the pain of separation (tragedy) or we eventually resolve the conflict and experience the excitement of a new level of harmony (comedy).

Please note that I make a distinction between the *drama* of life and the *play* of life. When we're involved in the *drama*, we become totally immersed in a particular conflict. Of course we, ourselves, are always the protagonist (good guy) while the *other person* is the antagonist (bad guy). We perceive things in terms of polarities: for/against, win/lose, succeed/fail, poverty/wealth, friend/enemy. We feel separate. We repeat old scripts. We struggle. Often there appears to be no way to resolve the problem. Stuck in the past and worried about the future, we fail to see humor in our situation. Life appears to be a farce, a melodrama, or a tragedy. And tragedy is usually what we fear most, for it implies suffering, humiliation, defeat, pain, confusion.

Suffering has a direct and powerful effect in helping the soul to ascend and to become free.
ROBERTO ASSAGIOLI

However, when we're involved in the *play* of life, we somehow remember that we are more than the parts we are playing. We see through the illusion of separateness and recognize the larger truth in the conflict. We can even decide which roles to take, because we aren't defined by any one part. Living in the moment, we are able to keep our hearts open to all of the people involved in the situation. We see humor in our human foibles and remind ourselves that every experience is part of a Divine Comedy. This means that we can *observe* the show and at the same time *participate fully.* We can feel all the pain and pleasure of the human drama without losing ourselves or without suffering so much. Then, standing by those who do take the Play too seriously, we can offer true compassion and understanding.

Our world is a great creative play.
JOSEPH CHILTON PEARCE

All the World's a Stage

In William Shakespeare's play *As You Like It,* the character Jaques makes the statement, "All the world's a stage and all the men and women merely players. They have their exits and their entrances and one man in his time plays many parts." Indeed, we're all players on the World Stage; we're all part of the same Drama. We touch each other's lives even though we may never meet face-to-face.

This "touching phenomenon" became apparent when Princess Diana died and we all stopped to mourn her passing. It was the first time in history when so many of us attended the same funeral. In the ruin of her life, we saw the frailties of our own aspirations. She was the beautiful, imperfect superstar of our Performance and she exited too soon.

The week following Diana's death, another one of our beloved stars left the Earth stage. In her life, Mother Teresa worked with the dying in Calcutta's ghettos, where she saw "the face of Christ" in every homeless person. In the quietness of her service, she reflected back to us the nobility of our own aspirations. She was the old, wrinkled saint of our Performance and we celebrated her full life when she made her exit—a more timely one in comparison to Diana's.

As actors on the World's Stage, we want to enjoy the Play on Earth and contribute something important. But often we stumble over our

Everyone alive is an actor but almost everyone alive is a very pathetic actor.
WILLIAM SAROYAN

lines or fake our way through the scenes. Most of us players don't know how to turn daily dramas into divine comedies.

While you can put down your newspaper and turn off your television, radio, and computer to shut out the drama in the outer world, you can't switch off *your own dramas within*! You can't escape the cacophony of inner voices that push and pull you in different directions, voices that want to know who you are, where you're going, and what the show's all about. The problem is this: If you don't know how to deal with the inner tumult, life can be hell.

Hell isn't fun. To be stuck in your private anguish is tragic drama. That's why I've written this book—to pull you from your inner hell, guide you through purgatory, and lead you into paradise. In *The Divine Comedy*, Dante Alighieri explored the depths and heights of consciousness and experienced every nuance of human expression, from the most vile in his *inferno* to the most sublime in his *paradiso*. It was the *inner quality* of a person that determined whether he or she sank to the abyss or ascended to the heavens.

Ah, but a man's reach should exceed his grasp, Or what's a heaven for?
ROBERT BROWNING

Perhaps you find yourself somewhere in between. Wherever you are, I invite you to make your play on Earth more enjoyable, meaningful, and worthwhile! Don't settle for routine, mediocre dramas. *Soul Play* can assist you in fine-tuning your character—or more precisely, your *inner characters*, and can guide you *safely* through expanded regions of consciousness.

The Inner Theatre Metaphor

Soul Play uses the metaphor of the "Inner Theatre" to represent your life: all of the physical, emotional, mental, and spiritual elements; your entire psychological world; and all that takes place inside your mind. Certainly there are many other metaphors for life, but the one I've found to be most useful comes from the theatre. Theatre itself, because it reflects the dynamic essence of characters drawn from everyday life, is one of the most powerful ways we have to explore and attempt to understand the individual, the world, and the individual's place in the world. This is surely why plays have been popular for thousands of years. They reflect reality back to us.

In stimulating our personal exploration, the theatre evokes deep emotions, often emotions that were previously unknown to us, and it externally personifies the inner drives and forces that cause us to do the things we do, things that often set people and society at odds with one another. The metaphor of the *Inner Theatre* provides you with a way to identify and resolve issues on your own inner stage, and to do so when that resolution may seem impossible in the outer world. You are given a way to direct your psychological energies, to work with the elements of your psyche, and to experience a deeper level of psychological integration, or *psycho-synthesis*.

While we know that metaphors are not literally the reality they describe—your inner life isn't *really* a theatre—metaphors use words and images to convey information about our lives and the world that *is* real. Visualizing the different parts of your personality as actors on the stage of your life can truly help you see your experience in a valuable new way.

Because metaphors stimulate imagination and intuition, they make it easy for the unconscious mind to communicate with the conscious mind. In a nonthreatening way, metaphors give you insight about yourself on various levels. And because these ideas and images come from *within you*, you are easily able to realize that they carry significant information about you, for you. That's the reason you will find that accepting the truth of these insights is easy and fun.

Metaphors, with great efficiency and amazing ease, involve your whole brain. While the left hemisphere (the so-called "left brain") is busy analyzing meaning and arranging all the pieces of the puzzle, your right hemisphere (or "right brain") perceives the *patterns* of your life and allows you to see the whole picture instantly. By combining analysis and synthesis, a metaphor cuts through rationalization, prejudice, and resistance, thereby communicating its message to you directly and incisively! This is a powerful, rapid, entertaining way to change and grow!

Take the metaphor of the *director*, for instance. In thinking of a director, you may see an image of a person in a director's chair. Or you may visualize a man or woman authoritatively giving instructions to the actors on stage. You might see a person earnestly holding private conversations with different actors, giving them advice and counsel. Perhaps you will see a person alone in an office, studying the script of a play, figuring out all the details of the production—how, when, and where the actors will move and speak. Regardless of what you may see the director doing, you can realize that there is a director within *you*. You, as director, may be accomplished and skillful in directing or you may lack the skills you need to put together a forceful performance. In either case, once you realize that *you are the director*, you're on your way to being able to work effectively with the parts of yourself and to develop self-mastery.

To me, what most clearly symbolizes the director's leadership position is the *director's chair*, an image to which I will return again and again in this book. When you imagine yourself taking charge of your inner drama, that director's chair is exactly where you will be sitting. In thinking about this chair you may ask: "Where *is* my chair?" "Who's actually sitting in it?" "How do I take leadership in my own theatre?" Those are questions to which you'll find answers in this book.

Overview

Here's a brief overview of what you'll find in *Soul Play*. First, you'll consider the connection between your soul and your play on Earth, and the reason why it's so easy to forget who you are. Then you'll exercise your imagination and prepare for an exciting inner adventure. You'll meet your "entourage"—your inner actors, director, and playwright, as well as members of your supporting cast and those in your audience. Then you'll take a tour of your inner theatre and explore the set. You'll see what's happening on stage and behind the scenes. You'll explore the basement and the upstairs (which I call the *mysterium*).

After all that, you'll discover your director's inner sanctum and find your director's chair. Most importantly, you'll learn the secrets of *who you are* and *what you do* as the director. You'll also make contact with the playwright—a very exciting get-together in which many people never consciously participate! Using what I call the "three steps in directing," you'll have the opportunity to take one of your unaccomplished actors through all three steps to help him or her become a star. To enhance that actor's new script, you and the playwright will explore how the role can be *even better*. Having practiced using the principles of directing, you'll realize that you now know how to work with the other actors to *get your act together.*

No man is free who is not master of himself.
EPICTETUS
FREED SLAVE, 90 A.D.

Imagination is the eye of the soul.
JOSEPH JOUBERT

Finally, you'll focus on the value of rehearsals and look more closely at the dark times in your life. You'll learn what to do when nothing seems to work and the stage appears empty. You'll discover what it means to give a peak performance and to enjoy each moment. And before completion, you'll also reflect on the roles you play in the Family, Organizational, and Community Theatres, and determine how *your* role fits into the larger World Play.

Now, before we actually begin, I want to answer some questions you may have.

Why read this book? What is its purpose?

This is not just another book to add to your collection. Instead, *Soul Play* is a call from your own soul to step back and take a deeper look at what your play in life is all about. It's a call to shift your perspective from the dramatic elements of your story to the reality of who you are behind your masks. It's a call to develop your character and to express your many star qualities.

Soul Play will help you develop self-awareness, self-acceptance, and self-mastery. In reading this book, *you,* as one of the world's actors, can expect to become the director of your own life, so you can play a more excellent part in the greater Performance.

For whom is the book written?

For *you.* Whether you are an engineer, factory worker, therapist, teacher, artist, CEO, mystic, or student, this book is meant for you. It's written for alert and concerned actors on the World Stage. Since everyone is involved in the Play, all who are interested in taking charge of their dramas can benefit, regardless of age, race, creed, or culture.

What are the underlying principles or traditions of this book?

The book reflects the elements of *Psychosynthesis*, a "psychology with a soul," developed by Italian psychiatrist Roberto Assagioli (1888-1974). In Psychosynthesis, the parts of the personality are singled out so one can understand their nature and their relationships (analysis) and then bring them together to express the fullness and beauty of the whole self (synthesis). This rich yet relatively unknown psychology offers a comprehensive approach to personal, transpersonal and social development. In fact, it was Assagioli's monograph *Life as a Game and Stage Performance* that inspired me to develop the Inner Theatre metaphor.

Overall and most important, *Soul Play* is based on principles of divine light, love, and will, and is for that reason *spiritual*. In addition, because it is . . .

. . . based on principles of education, it is *instructive*;

. . . based on principles of psychology, it is *therapeutic;*

. . . based on principles of energy medicine, it is *healing;*

. . . based on principles of directing and acting, it is *entertaining*.

The Inner Theatre approach sounds intriguing, but how does it actually work?

Imagine watching your daily drama from an objective perspective. At work, the office is your stage. Your desk, computer, and papers are your props. You're dressed in your usual business costume. Today your boss is condescending and impatient with you and other workers. In turn, you're angry, resentful, and a bit worried. You know this old drama by heart and it isn't fun. Suddenly you remember that your Businessperson is just one of your actors playing a part. You step back from this role and take your director's chair. What if you, as the director, helped your actor change his lines, or what if you brought in Monsieur Diplomat to help deal with the boss? How could you make this scene turn out differently?

Or it's the end of the day and you arrive home dead tired and hungry. The stage is now set in the living room, where your spouse is reading the newspaper and watching television, not contributing to the household tasks. You point this out. Soon both of you are arguing about fairness and rights. Will the same old song and dance replay or will one of you step back from your role-as-spouse and take your director's chair to address the problem on another level?

The time is now midnight and the scene shifts to the bedroom. Who will appear in the spotlight tonight? Will your seductive Lover invite your partner's passionate Lover to bed, or will your whimpering inner Child crawl under the sheets to snuggle with your mate's reassuring inner Parent? Who will determine who goes to bed with whom?

After a moment's reflection, you can think of other examples, such as the tragic Drama of Joint Custody, which often takes place when parents drop off or pick up their children. Incriminations and excuses are exchanged for approximately twenty or thirty minutes before the parents depart in despair and mutual loathing. Where's the director here? Who can help the Ex-spouse actor heal the pain and begin to love once again? Who can help design a new ending to this totally frustrating script?

Will I benefit if I simply read the book and don't do the exercises?

As with everything else, the benefits you receive will depend on the degree of commitment you have to developing your inner life. If you're embroiled in conflict and are suffering, you can use the exercises in this book to lead you through the difficulties. Change won't happen overnight, but it will come about if you are committed to helping yourself. If you're *not* committed, your struggling actors will continue to scream, scratch, and bleed all over your stage. As you know, slipping and sliding in your own blood is melodramatic and very painful! I recommend that you make the effort to change.

If you are healthy and your life is fairly functional, you may use the program in this book to *fine-tune* your presentation. As any accomplished musician knows, an instrument that is a *little* out of tune can ruin an otherwise superb performance. Your inner actors will thank you for the time and attention you give to polishing their roles. This is true "character development."

Finally, if you are one of the lucky few whose life flows smoothly most of the time, you can extend your possibilities even further and create new scripts with the gods and goddesses themselves. In the Theatre of the Divine, there are no limitations to the expansion of consciousness! Yours is a Never-Ending Story.

What does the author want readers to get from this book?

My deepest desire is that you remember who you are behind all of your masks. By knowing who you are and giving the best of yourself, you will become a better person, and the world will become a better place to be.

I hope you'll find *Soul Play* inspiring, intimate, and liberating. Read this book for the fun of it. Read it to increase your joy. Read it to put more life in your Life!

Now, if you're ready, I'll step aside and raise the curtain. Enjoy the show!

Raising the Curtain

The Soul's Masquerade

Settling back in the most comfortable seat in the house, you watch as the curtain rises, revealing scenes from *Cocoon*, the film by Ron Howard. *You are there*, and you watch as an enterprising skipper finds himself attracted to a slender young woman who, along with several male companions, has rented his yacht for a special diving mission.

You smell the sea breezes as you watch the woman go below deck to her chamber on a balmy afternoon. Magnetized by her presence, the skipper goes to her door and quietly crouches outside, peering through the keyhole. He watches as she undresses slowly and gracefully. She is tan and beautiful. Then just as naturally as she removes her clothing, she reaches up behind her neck, slips off her hair and face, and proceeds to step out of her skin. Dropping her human costume on the floor, she scintillates as a light and shining being. The skipper, totally stunned by what he sees, meets her gaze through the peephole—then runs away in a panic.

The woman in the film has an earthly mission that requires a human body, but—you realize as the story develops—she never forgets that she is more than her skin. The skipper on the other hand, believes something is "terribly wrong" with *her* and forgets that he, too, is a radiant being in a human costume.

Italian philosopher Tommaso Campanella wrote a sonnet that begins like this: "In the theatre of the world our souls play a masquerade, hiding themselves behind their bodies and effects."

In the theatre of the world *our soul plays a masquerade*! It's all a grand Divine Comedy! Perhaps we could say that the soul joins the great Actors' Guild of the Human Race when it takes a physical body and is born on Earth. Having access to the Costume Department, the luminous Self chooses a guise for the masquerade. It may hide behind skin that is rose beige, creamy brown, medium olive, velvet black, or ivory porcelain. It may choose to take a male or female form for its human incarnation.

Cultural and religious choices are multiple. One's soul may arrive in a nomad's tent in the Sahara desert, a maharajah's palace in India, a

The soul is the essence of who you are.
BILLY GRAHAM

When the soul wishes to experience something, she simply throws out an image and enters into it.
MEISTER ECKHART

*The Unnameable has
given you this shape
to Play, to Love,
to Know Thy Self.
Don't forget this!*
SRI H. W. L. POONJA

*The soul plays the self
as a consummate stage
actor plays a character
—with detachment and
total involvement at the
same time.*
GABRIELLE ROTH

jet-setter's apartment in Paris, a farmhouse in Kansas. The family it is born into may be religious or agnostic, or somewhere in between.

What generally happens in infancy is that families or tribe members begin to relate to the newborn exclusively as a physical being and forget to see the soul shining through. Then, if the baby's inner light is not reflected back, the little one soon forgets that he or she is a *divine being*.

You know the rest of the story. As we grow up, we put on social masks and elaborate costumes to fit in with those around us. We find ourselves playing many different parts. We hide who we really are because we're afraid we're not good enough. We're afraid we'll be judged, "found out," rejected.

Slowly we begin to identify with the parts we play and then believe we *are* those parts. Some people don't just *play* the roles of Pleaser, Parent, Politician, or Pimp; they think they *are* the roles. Some don't just *wear* the masks of Wage-Earner, Warrior, Worrier, or Wimp; they believe they *are* the masks.

Throughout the day we express many aspects of ourselves. That is natural. However, when we get stuck in a role or when we believe we have no choice but to perform an old song and dance, we suffer. And sometimes we suffer big time.

Why, we wonder, did the soul choose this human experience? Why is it playing a masquerade?

We might think of it this way. A novelist gets an idea for a new story one day while she's looking idly out her window. She sits at her computer (for she is a modern woman) and begins to develop the plot and characters. As she works, the story begins to take on a life of its own in her mind. The characters begin to tell her who *they* are and what *they* want. Relationships among them are established. Intriguing conflicts are created. The exciting and entertaining plot thickens to keep readers in suspense. Then finally the mysteries are resolved; the tensions are broken. Whether it turns out to be a tragedy or a comedy, the story is over. The End!

When she's finished, the author realizes to her surprise that she herself has changed. She now knows herself in ways she never could have before. Through her creation, she discovers more of who she is.

In much the same way, we may imagine that the soul, desiring to know itself in multiple dimensions, chooses to become human and experience its own "novel." In human form, the soul experiences all the dualities and polarities of earthly life and discovers its own various facets and nuances.

Why do we forget who we are?

Perhaps we forget who we are so we can really get into the story, get into it in a way we couldn't if we were not fully involved in the material world. Perhaps we desire to experience the thrill of remembering. Do you recall the excitement of playing hide-and-seek when you were young? Can you still hear the shrieks of delight when you were *found*?

Getting lost and finding ourselves makes great drama. It's the theme that runs through many of the world's great literary classics, including *Quest for the Holy Grail* (England), *Ramayana* (India), and *Kuan Yin* (China). It includes Dante's *Divine Comedy* (Italy), Homer's *Odyssey* (Greece), Dostoyevski's *The Brothers Karamazov* (Russia), and Baum's *The Wizard of Oz* (America).

As a modern-day person performing your own version of the play, will you remember that getting lost, though part of the great drama, is only an illusion? Will you remember who you have always been? Those are the questions!

The self is forgotten so it can be remembered. It's the Play.
GANGAJI

There is no finding the self. You are that self!
RAMANA MAHARSHI

On Imagination Street

To attend the Masquerade Ball on earth, the soul agrees to live a dual existence—to live in both the inner and outer worlds simultaneously.

The inner and outer worlds are both real and significant. They are dynamic and ever-changing. Both attempt to maintain integrity and equilibrium as they interact with each other. While most people find it easy to make their way around the well-mapped outer world (the reality in front of their eyes), few know how to find their way in the inner world (the reality behind their eyes). For many, the inner regions remain a mystery.

Moving inward, we discover infinity. Here there are no barriers, no boundaries, no restraints, no time limits. If we choose, we can fly to the farthest reaches of the galaxy in the sky of mind.

To get the most out of the Earth experience, we must take time to understand and develop our inner life. As the Swiss philosopher and poet Henri Frederic Amiel noted, "The man who has no inner life is a slave to his surroundings." To assure that you're not one of the enslaved, you need to find time to be alone and to reflect inwardly, even though finding the time may be hard. Developing your inner life is deeply rewarding on every level. Besides, you get to take all your inner riches with you when you die—an added bonus. The time you reserve for yourself will definitely pay off in the long run.

To discover your inner domain, you must use your imagination and have a spirit of adventure. The great theoretical physicist Albert Einstein once said, "Imagination is more powerful than knowledge." *Why did he say that?* Could it be that imagination is more powerful because it activates the creative function of the mind, while knowledge simply activates the memory?

For a moment, use your imagination and envision yourself standing on the corner of Imagination Street and Adventure Avenue. Now imagine that Knowledge is standing on one side of you (hands filled with books) and Imagination is standing on the other (hands empty and free). Both beckon you to follow.

When you walk along with Knowledge, you discover that he is happy to assist you by offering important facts and figures related to

Infinite worlds appear and disappear in the vast expanse of my own consciousness.
ANCIENT VEDIC SAYING

Some people accuse Imagination of being a liar. They don't understand that she has her own ways of uncovering the truth.
J. RUTH GENDLER

your physical perceptions and the material world. He's also great with pragmatic problem-solving. However, you can get a bit tired after a while because he keeps talking on and on. Under your breath you may say impatiently, "I know, I know." You also have to be careful that he doesn't ask you to carry all his excess baggage. (He doesn't travel light!)

When the two of you are together, Indoctrination is apt to join you. Indoctrination thinks he knows it all and tries to structure your mind so you'll believe only what he wants you to believe. He's militantly determined that he's right! This, of course, makes you wrong if you express a thought of your own. When he's around, you begin to feel small and unimportant, and find you don't have much to say.

On the other hand, when you walk down the path with Imagination, Intuition soon joins you. Those two take you to places where thoughts, ideas, and images are born. When you're with them, you feel alive and excited. You feel free to ask questions, to dream, to play, and to create. With them, you don't get tired.

In your inner theatre, Imagination and Intuition help you use your "mind's eye" to see, your "mind's ear" to hear, your "mind's nose" to smell, your "mind's tongue" to taste, and your "mind's skin" to touch. They help you develop these extrasensory perceptions that are subtler than your five physical senses.

Along the way, you'll also meet Venture, juggling his maps and traveling paraphernalia. When he shakes your hand, you'll discover what a real handshake feels like. With an enormous smile and great enthusiasm, he assures you that he can help you find amazing places and treasures within.

Then there's Pleasure, who's wild and sweet; and Panache, who's gallant and flamboyant. In a sweeping gesture, Panache bows low in a grand Renaissance inflect, while Pleasure offers you fresh cherries in an elegant cloisonné bowl.

Grace also greets you and invites you to take off your coat and hat and armor and masks. She encourages you to lay down your sword and laptop computer and briefcase and purse. She gives you permission to go barefoot and to let your hair blow in the wind!

The world of reality has its limits; the world of imagination is boundless.
JEAN-JACQUES ROUSSEAU

I shut my eyes in order to see.
PAUL GAUGUIN

Yes, in your inner explorations you'll find these companions and many more. All are prepared to take you to various regions of consciousness where you will discover vast resources available to you. But first they are prepared to help you get acquainted with your very own entourage—the voices you hear inside your mind.

Discovering Who's Who

The Entourage

On the corner of Imagination Street and Adventure Avenue, in the theatre of your mind, you will find a cast of characters as rich and varied as those portrayed on a Broadway stage.

But who are they? Who are the *dramatis personae* in your inner theatre? *Who's who* in your production?

Although you are one person, your one self has many parts. Just as one diamond has many facets and one rainbow has many colors, your personality has many aspects and nuances. Truly, you are a multi-dimensional being!

In your entourage, you'll find a teeming *cast of characters* all voicing their opinions about how you should live your life. These different inner actors compete for attention, telling you how to act, where to go, how to think, what to feel. At times you are encouraged and inspired by these voices; at other times you are confused or impatient with their chatter.

You'll also find a *director* in your inner theatre. How well your play is performed on Earth depends on your director's ability to take charge of your actors and help them develop their "character."

And, of course, you'll also find a *playwright* inspiring your performance. This playwright is your soul, creating the script for your masquerade. Indeed, one can say that in your inner theatre, you are the playwright, the director, and all the players! Essentially, your whole life is your play!

But that's not all. You are a part of something much bigger than your individual self. You also have an *audience*, made up of all those who observe your life, and a *supporting cast*, consisting of beings who have something special to offer your show. Then there's the *Universal Playwright*—the scriptwriter for *all* Plays.

To clarify how the entourage fits in with terms you may already know, consider the following correlations:

It is time to explain myself. Let us stand up.
WALT WHITMAN

*Do I contradict myself?
Very well then
I contradict myself.
I am large.
I contain multitudes.*
WALT WHITMAN

Inner Theatre	*Religion*	*Psychosynthesis*
⇓	⇓	⇓
Universal Playwright	God	Universal Self
playwright	soul	transpersonal Self
director	self	personal self
actors	parts	subpersonalities

Let's continue as I introduce you to the members of your entourage, beginning with your actors. As we go on, you'll have the opportunity to experience every facet of yourself in more depth.

The Actors

Each of us is a crowd," says my friend and Psychosynthesis colleague Piero Ferrucci in his book *What We May Be*. In speaking about the cast of characters, he explains: "There can be the rebel and the intellectual, the seducer and the housewife, the saboteur and the aesthete, the organizer and the bon vivant—each with its own mythology, and all more or less comfortably crowded into one single person." He goes on to add, "Often they are far from being at peace with one another."

This motley cast represents the various roles we play in life and our typical patterns of behavior. Like the cells in a body, they are distinct, yet all connected. Each colorful actor is like a miniature personality (also called a *subpersonality*) with a mind, heart, and will of its own.

For example, the actors most active in my own life at this time include the reclusive Writer and Editor, who work side-by-side at my computer; my Financier, who tries to juggle the cast's priorities; the Mom, who lives too far from her grown son; the devoted Daughter, Sister, and Aunt, all of whom jump into the car every so often and drive to Kansas to visit the family; and of course the Educator, who travels at home and abroad to give workshops. After many years of working together, they live quite peacefully together and support one another in the best ways they can. Occasionally the Cook complains that she isn't given the time to be more creative.

After being introduced to the concept of inner actors during one of my workshops, Edward, a Protestant minister in his thirties, stayed up late that night to identify some of the most prominent players on his stage. The next morning he enthusiastically introduced us to those who appeared in his spotlight. Among the fifteen he mentioned were:

Dr. Statesman: The totally serious aristocrat, a slightly pompous lecturer and leader.

Gremlin: The fat friar, who tries desperately to satisfy his emotional needs with food.

Goofy: The clown, who is always on stage and loves being the center of attention.

Harmony: The sweet, sexy, feminine singer of love songs.

The mystic is the divine child in us all wanting to play in the universe.
MATTHEW FOX

In every one of us there lies a sleeping beauty waiting to be awakened through love.
SARAH B. BREATHNACH

Freddy and Frieda Fear: The fear twins, who are afraid, respectively, of prosperity and poverty, illness and abundant health, rejection and acceptance, etc. and etc.

Leo: The lionhearted lover, who accepts everyone and everything. He is the peacekeeper and protector. He is pure of heart, truly the king of the other actors.

As he shared his list, all of us in the workshop—including Edward—were able to see the degree to which a number of his inner actors were quite different from Rev. Minister, the main actor in Edward's inner theatre.

There's a martial artist in me who comes straight from the Shaolin temples.
ADAM CHRISTOPHER

Actors want to be heard, so they try to get attention in amazing ways. If you stop to listen, you might hear them whisper, cry, scream, complain, coax, or make snide remarks. Some may argue or contradict you. Others may blurt out embarrassing statements in public.

Let me tell you about Kathy. A talented lawyer and musician, Kathy felt that an important inner part of her was being held captive. By what or by whom, she wasn't sure. But, having discovered her own inner theatre, she knew she could call her "captive" onto the stage. When she did, who should appear in her imagination but—*Wild Woman*. Wild Woman was disheveled, confused, and sad. In her remarks to Kathy, she said she had been locked in the basement for years.

And who was *Wild Woman*?

Wild Woman was a highly energetic, creative aspect of Kathy, whose job was to express herself; in fact, Kathy's very soul depended on the freedom of this expression. Years ago, however, someone had slammed the door of creativity in Wild Woman's face, and she was made a hostage. Oh yes, there were times when Kathy—unconsciously giving expression to Wild Woman—would engage in bouts of wanton and lustful sex, or would drink and use drugs. Her involvement in these activities was the only way she knew to use this incredible, boundless energy that for some reason was being stifled.

Inside you there is an artist you don't know about.
RUMI, SUFI POET

Over time, the creative flame that defined Kathy's soul diminished. Without fully realizing what was going on, Kathy posted a guard in her own mind to keep Wild Woman in check. Her doing so was supported by her general impression of how a woman was "supposed to act."

Years passed, yet the flame was not entirely extinguished. It still flickered. Then suddenly, Wild Woman was invited onto the stage and she stood there dazed, not sure where she was or who had called her out.

Like Kathy, you no doubt are aware that you have inner actors who aren't being fully honored and acknowledged. Whether you like it or not, they demand attention, love, fame, wealth, power—you name it, they'll demand it. They plead with you, tempt you, and even get you to do things you wouldn't ordinarily do if you were in your "right mind."

Actors often give conflicting messages. Philosopher Sam Keen described the inner confusion when he said: "I fear my inner guru may be senile. He offers contradictory advice: take it easy/work harder, risk everything/stay where you are, dare madness/cultivate sanity. He can never decide if he is on the side of Dionysus or Apollo."

In time, you discover that you have both *accomplished* and *unaccomplished* actors living inside. "Some are dark and formidable, some radiant with light, but all are complexities of lively energy," says Gretchen Sliker in her book *Multiple Mind.*

In a very real sense, we know what it's like to have the whole world live within us. Philosopher Hermann Keyserling stated: "In each of us can be found, developed and active in various proportions, all instincts, all passions, all vices and virtues, all tendencies and aspirations, all faculties and endowments of mankind."

As human beings, we all share similar thoughts, feelings, and experiences, yet each of us develops a totally unique cast! While we have the *potential* to play every possible role, from Hitler to Mother Teresa, not every character is birthed or developed in each person. Also, different situations evoke different parts of our personality. For example, the Defender won't appear unless someone is threatening you. The Lover won't show up unless an attractive or interesting person enters the stage. Sue Perior won't flaunt her stuff unless there are people around upon whom she can look down. And players such as the Alcoholic or the Glutton won't appear on your marquee unless they are wined and dined on a regular basis.

Others, however, such as the Child, Adolescent, and Parent, are active in all of us and often appear in the spotlight. It's not uncommon for my barefooted, pigtailed, little country Girl to beg me to climb our

In each of us there is a King. Speak to him and he will come forth!
SCANDINAVIAN PROVERB

In every real man a child is hidden that wants to play.
FRIEDRICH NIETZSCHE

apple trees. Occasionally I climb with her, and my inner Mom tells me to be careful and not go too high. She's always afraid I might fall.

You may wonder if giving attention to your actors could make you feel fragmented or crazy. For most of us, it clearly won't! We naturally exhibit different parts of our personality all the time: from being a Dummy in one area to a real Genius in another; from being a selective Shopper at the supermarket to a slick Salesperson at the PTA Bazaar. All human beings everywhere have multiple parts to their personality, so having many parts doesn't make one emotionally unbalanced. In fact, a growing body of evidence from psychological and medical research strongly suggests that the more we understand our multiplicity, the more we increase our cognitive abilities and emotional capacities. It's time to celebrate the rich diversity within ourselves!

✎ *Who are the actors most prominent in your play at this time?*

AND MORE

After dinner, the group
of such disparate occupations
made up a kind
of unofficial game,
played idly, lazily
and only half in jest:
"If you were not what you are,
what would you like to be?"
"An artist," one said promptly,
"A singer," said another.

And then the categories
flew with lightning speed:
composer, actor, talk show host,
architect, dancer, navigator,
composer, prospector—
and something in me:
the child for whom
there had never been
enough yeses—
the one in whose lexicon
there was no word for enough
            cried silently:
Don't stop. Keep talking.
I want to be all,
all of those—
and more.

— *E.B. de Vito*

The Director

Actors need a director to make the most of their talents and activities. In the inner theatre, *you* are the director-self—the governing center of your personality. This is your human self in time and space—the one responsible for orchestrating your life on Earth. As director, you're the organizing center. You're more than all your actors or roles.

For example, I, Vivian, am my director-self—the human me who's responsible for my daily show. As director, I have the task of recognizing my actors, unifying the ensemble, and producing the play. I am the one who senses the direction my play will take. By creating an atmosphere in which my actors can experiment with their roles, I allow the underlying theme of my play to be uncovered and expressed. Essentially, I am responsible for my personal performance.

You may mentally understand the concept of a director, but to actually *feel in charge of your life* takes practice. Many people have no idea who they are as the directing self, which is why we witness so many poor performances. For most, no one's in charge and the play just "happens." You could say the director is away on vacation, out to lunch, or even asleep.

What is the difference between the actors and the director?

Perhaps you can answer this question for yourself in the following exercise.

To be or not to be: that is the question.
SHAKESPEARE

Every man must be his own leader. He must follow the light that's within himself . . .
LAURENS VAN DER POST

Director and Actors

✍ *Write down the names of three inner actors who play central roles in your life.*

Bring the first actor into focus. Who is it? How does it act? What does it wear? What does it contribute to the show?

Imagine what your play would be like if this actor never played another part in your life. What if it disappeared from the stage and never returned? What would be missing? What would be gained?

Next, bring the second actor into focus. Who is it? What does it do? What does this part talk about? How important is this actor to the cast? What does it contribute to the show?

You are not a personality, even though you wear a personality. Perhaps you wear it so tightly that you have overlooked that if you drop it, you remain whole and full, while it lies lifeless on the floor.
GANGAJI

Imagine what your play would be like if this actor left the stage and didn't return for some reason. How would your life be different?

Now bring the third actor into focus. Who is it? What role does it play? What important quality does it bring to the show?

Consider what your life would be like if this actor left, never to play another part in your drama. What would life be like? What would be missing?

As the director, the one in charge of the performance, consider this: Without these three actors, who would you be? If you didn't play these roles, would you cease to exist? Of course not, but your play would change dramatically. Who, then, is the you that is more than your roles—more than your actors?

Now remember that because you're the director, you're free to choose which actors play roles in your drama. Since you're the one in charge, you can ask them all to come back and participate if you wish. You can decide who takes the spotlight, and when. As director, you're free to choose the roles that are played.

Undress yourself of these things and find where "I" rises from.
SRI H. W. L. POONJA

The director is who you are after you have taken off all your costumes and masks. It's who you are when you stand psychologically naked, stripped of all identifications. You are more than your characters or characteristics. Although you can step back from a mask or role, you can never step back from your self. The director-self is who you are when you can't step back any farther.

✍ Who do you think is in charge of your show at this time in life? Is your director active on the set, out to lunch, or away on vacation? Explain.

The Playwright

If there's a play, there must be a playwright. Right? Who is the playwright in your inner theatre? Do you have a sense of who's inspiring your show?

The playwright is your invisible Self—the spirit behind your human form, the "soul who plays a masquerade." Because your playwright is invisible, you cannot see, feel, measure, or weigh this dimension of yourself. Nevertheless, this greater You is substantial and real. Many people are unaware of their soul because they can't define or study it with ordinary, rational, scientific tools and methods.

Those who don't know the playwright are unaware of their essential nature. Since they are not in contact with the scriptwriter, they tend to produce superficial, sensational, or mediocre dramas. In fact, *mediocrity is evidence that a performance lacks soul.*

The playwright is the one who shapes your life and creates your human script. Just as a novelist conceives of the characters in a book and gets to know each one intimately, your playwright envisions the parts of your personality, animates each character, and establishes the theme that runs through your entire play. Once created, inner actors take on a life of their own as they interact with one another. And while actors come and go like characters in a morning soap opera, your playwright-Self remains steady, sure, and always available.

Be assured that you are very important to your playwright. *Why?* Because the playwright needs the director—the human self—to orchestrate the play on Earth. Without a director, actors run the show, creating chaos, turmoil, and suffering. The playwright is also very important to you. *Why?* Because you need the playwright to inspire, guide, and reveal the larger purpose of your performance.

To get acquainted with your playwright, begin by talking to your Self in the same way that you would talk to a friend. You can even ask its name. For example, I call my playwright "Viva," a name that came to me when I asked for one in meditation. We now call each other "Viva" and "Vivian" instead of "playwright" and "director." This makes our relationship more personal and less technical; more real and less conceptual.

But sometimes we go to a play and after the curtain has been up five minutes we have a sense of being able to settle back in the arms of the playwright. Instinctively we know the playwright knows his business.
THE SELECTED LETTERS OF
ANTON CHEKHOV

Your soul is an inner universe: infinite, mysterious, powerful.
THOMAS MOORE

Remember, the playwright, director, and actors are all different dimensions of your one Self. Each has a distinctly different perspective and quality of energy, but is not separate from you. You are much more than you think you are! If this all seems a bit confusing, don't be concerned. This is simply an introduction, and you'll have many more opportunities to clarify these dimensions of yourself as we go along.

✍ *Are you aware of your playwright-Self? If your playwright had a name, what might it be?*

The Universal Playwright

Our individual playwright is not Supreme Reality. No, our playwright has high-level connections with a much Greater Being—the *Universal Playwright*.

The consciousness of this Great One is responsible for the Cosmic Production and inspires all sentient beings to reach their potential. This One holds the pattern, or divine script, for what actors from all nations, cultures, races, and galaxies can become.

Physician and renowned teacher Deepak Chopra explains it this way in *The Seven Spiritual Laws of Success*: "The universal mind choreographs everything that is happening in billions of galaxies with elegant precision and unfaltering intelligence. Its intelligence is ultimate and supreme, and it permeates every fiber of existence; from the smallest to the largest, from the atom to the cosmos."

Our Universal Playwright is said to have a thousand names and faces, some of which are the *Creative Power of the Universe*, the *unified field of consciousness*, *the Implicate Order*, and the *Source*. Names given by the world's religions include the following:

American Indians	Great Spirit
Buddhism	Buddha
Christianity	God
Hinduism	Ishvara
Islam	Allah
Judaism	Adonai Elohim
Taoism	The Tao

Many people today, in an attempt to transcend the dualistic notion that God is of one gender or the other, prefer to address the Divine as *God/Goddess/All That Is*.

People sometimes ask me where I think Christ fits into all this. My personal belief (influenced by my Christian background) is that Christ is intimately involved in helping to make our planet a sacred Play through the processes of evolution, renewal, and resurrection of the Spirit. Once, as a human being on Earth, he showed us what it's like to have *the human act together*. He lived with his spirit *unmasked* and

God, that made the world and all things. . . . He is not far from every one of us: For in him we live and move, and have our being.
ACTS 17: 24, 27-28

. . . wherever ye turn, there is God's face.
THE KORAN

The Infinite One is known by the name of Beauty.
DIONYSIUS THE AREOPAGITE

Nameless indeed is the source of creation, But things have a mother and she has a name.
LAO TZU

I find the notion of having a relationship with a deity you can think of as a mother profoundly healing.
RIANE EISLER

For I know the plans I have for you, plans for good and not for evil, to give you a future full of hope.
JEREMIAH 29:11

said we, too, could live that way. Nevertheless, from our human perspective, we obviously cannot understand what is *beyond understanding*. St. Paul said, "Now we are seeing a dim reflection in a mirror; but then we shall be seeing face to face. The knowledge that I have now is imperfect; but then I shall know as fully as I am known." (1 Corinthians 13:12, *Jerusalem Bible*)

As long as we're immersed in Earth's pageant, the Drama will often appear confusing and chaotic. However, as chaos theorists observe, there is a hidden order in chaos. The Universal Author is the creator of that order—a higher order—and knows the underlying purpose of the Universal Play. We can trust what is unfolding.

You are a child of the universe,
No less than the trees and the stars;
you have a right to be here.
And whether or not it is clear to you,
no doubt the universe is unfolding as it should.
                    —DESIDERATA

✍ *Do you have a name for the Universal Playwright? How much do you trust what is unfolding in your life's play?*

The Audience

People who observe or participate in your life make up your audience. This includes family, friends, relatives, co-workers, and neighbors. Just as they are the audience for your performance, you are the audience for theirs.

The audience gives you a purpose for acting. If no one shows interest in your life—if no one seems to care about your performance—your act will probably lack meaning and motivation. We are social beings. We don't live in a void.

Russian theatre director Constantin Stanislavski believed the audience provides "acoustics" for the performers. In other words, people who observe our daily actions serve as sounding boards. They give us *feedback* about what they like or don't like. The type of audience we have (the people we associate with from day to day) determines the frequency and quality of this feedback.

As a therapist, I remember a particular session I had with Blaine, a film critic from Los Angeles. He imagined looking out into his audience to identify those present. His wife, several journalists, and about six friends were sitting toward the front with apparent interest in what he was doing. His sister was sitting toward the back of the auditorium preoccupied with her child. On the left, his brother was smoking pot, quite oblivious to what was taking place on stage. His father was sleeping in the balcony.

The center seat in the front row was empty, an insight that disturbed Blaine intensely. With rising anger, he said: "That is the seat I have been saving for my mother all my life. She has never shown up! I keep thinking she will, but she refuses to come. I feel enraged and helpless."

Blaine's insight gave us valuable information that led to deeper emotional healing for him. In the sessions that followed, two things happened: First, he forgave his real mother for not being present. Second, he invited *the inner Mother he had always wanted* to take the center seat. This Mother (the Mother archetype) knew how his human mother had betrayed the original script. She knew how he had suffered.

Blaine shifted from despair to hope as he envisioned his inner Mother taking this seat of honor. With her in the center, he imagined what it was like to be seen by a Mother who lovingly applauds him.

There is no part of the world that is not looking at you.
RAINER MARIA RILKE

The audience is a creative participant in the performance of a play.
STANISLAVSKI

Later developments were even more satisfying. Five years later, his human mother appeared in his audience and apologized for not having been present before. Pleased but cautious, Blaine reports that he believes things are now changing for the two of them.

Surround yourself with people who respect and treat you well.
CLAUDIA BLACK

The audience may include those who are living on this Earth and those who have already left their bodies. For example, in my audience, my mom and dad sit in the front row, although my mom is no longer in her physical body, and my dad lives 500 miles away. Regardless of distance or time, I continue to feel their love and support.

Laurens van der Post spoke with poetic passion about those who no longer wear physical costumes. "We make a great mistake when we think that people whose lives have been intimately woven into our own, cease to influence us when they die," he said. "The dead become part of the dynamics of our spirit. They join the infinite ranks of the past, as vast as the hosts of the future, and so much greater than our own little huddle of people in the present."

Most of us can only see the "huddle of people in the present," but, in truth, more people are in our audience than we'll ever be aware of. Our daily dramas are observed by multitudes.

What about our responsibility to those in the audience?

As performers, we have a sacred responsibility to those who witness our lives. These are the questions we must address: How authentic are we acting? How fully do we give of ourselves to the audience?

Addressing the matter of the actor's loyalty to the audience, Polish theatre director Jerzy Grotowsk explained that we must discard "half measures"; we must reveal, open up, and emerge from ourselves rather than closing up. He believed that self-revelation "could be compared to an act of the most deeply rooted, genuine love between two human beings." This act he called "a total act."

A total act!

✍ *Consider the "acoustics" your audience provides. Who are the people in your audience and where do they sit? Do they encourage you to "act totally?" If you could change your audience, what would you change?*

The Supporting Cast

Directing is a big responsibility, but you don't have to do it all by yourself. In fact, you're better off if you don't. A whole supporting cast is on call.

Supporting members are guest stars who inspire and encourage you. They offer ideas, suggestions, and professional advice. They act as role models and influence the quality of your performance. These supporting members include:

Angels, spiritual masters, saints, sages, mystics, ministers;
Teachers, mentors, therapists, healers, consultants;
Coaches, twelve-step sponsors, advisors;
Ancestors, family, friends;
Artists, poets, musicians, authors;
Characters from movies, television shows, books;
Mythological gods/goddesses/characters, archetypes, muses;
Nature spirits, spirit animals, pets, devas, elves, fairies.

You get the point. You are not alone! In a magical, wonderful way, you have access to the wisdom and guidance of great ones throughout the ages—past, present, and future. You can invite members of this supporting cast onto your stage at any time, in any place, to help with any situation. They can serve as comforters, counselors, or consultants.

As director, you will need specialized help at times. If one of your actors is addicted, you may need to find the right twelve-step group. If your Adolescent is bulimic, you need to ask a physician and/or therapist for help. If your inner Accountant has money to invest, you may need to seek advice from an investment broker.

Perhaps you want to learn a new skill. How do you go about doing that? If your inner Athlete wants to learn golf, most likely you'll look for the best golf coach in town. I'm reminded of Tiger Woods, the famous young golf professional. His supporting cast includes his devoted parents and many accomplished coaches. Yes, he has great talent, but would he be where he is today without help from others? I doubt it.

I am with you always.
JESUS CHRIST

. . . there is nothing and nobody that you do not have access to, within your heart.
PTAAH

GREEK MUSES
Dominion (*leadership*)
Erato (*human relations*)
Fortuna (*commerce*)
Iris (*beauty*)
Juris (*justice, balance*)
Laurel (*teaching*)
Lumen (*writing*)
Lyra (*music*)
Oracle (*intuition*)
Persona (*performance*)
Vela (*discovery*)
Zoe (*healing*)

Angels and ministers of grace, defend us!
SHAKESPEARE

Actually, most of the members of your supporting cast are *unseen.* You won't find them in offices, sitting across from you at home, available to you on the phone, or being otherwise present in physical form at all. They are available in spirit form. Knowing that you have access to those who have been the greatest guides throughout the ages is exhilarating.

The supporting cast can give us help on every level, can help us with every need. A therapist who facilitates women's circles in Arizona has an inner council of goddesses whom she calls upon for guidance and strength. A sensuous blonde artist from Santa Fe often invites Mary Magdalene to discuss spiritual issues with her cast. Yet another woman, Margot Adler, the granddaughter of Austrian psychiatrist Alfred Adler, finds an active awareness of the goddess Athena useful. She recounts the time she negotiated a business contract and used the image of Athena as a way of becoming strong and standing up for what she needed.

According to Napoleon Hill, the author of *Think and Grow Rich,* holding internal conversations with role models is very useful. He discovered this when he interviewed successful entrepreneurs and found they did just that. To people who wanted to improve themselves, Hill suggested that they consciously create a group of "Invisible Counselors" from whom to seek advice. Well, why not? Why not have your own inner group of advisors? Personally, I invite Christ to be ever-present on my stage to help with my performance. Knowing he's working closely with my playwright gives me a deep sense of trust and inner peace.

Making contact with these inner teachers and guides can sometimes lead to exciting, unexpected later developments. Remember Kathy's Wild Woman? After being released from prison, Wild Woman felt the strong presence of a man in her inner theatre. Immediately she trusted him. When she asked who he was, he said simply, "Call me *The Man Who Isn't Afraid.*"

Wild Woman wanted to know more, so he whispered in her ear. "I have known you for quite some time. I am a teacher. I teach through the use of words and pictures, but mostly by example. I have been taught by many wise teachers, Wild Woman, including you. Now I would like to give something back. I know how energies flow magically when the intention is held that all things be offered for the highest good. I applaud the efforts, creations, and successes of others; yes, also of you, Wild Woman. I want to teach you to trust the flow of energies for your expression and creations. You need not be afraid. . . . You will never be alone, Wild Woman. I will always be here for you. All you need to do is call my name."

As Kathy tells it, Wild Woman believed him. "In her enthusiasm and excitement, Wild Woman began to dance on stage. She danced away years of restriction and repression. She danced away patterns of mediocrity and conformity. She danced away concerns of separation and isolation. She danced away old belief systems that no longer served her. The sun and the moon joined in. The flowers and the trees swayed with them. The oceans moved rhythmically, while the animals roared, snorted, and pawed the ground in solidarity. The whole world danced until dancing seemed like the only way to be."

How beautiful to be wild about life!

Our supporting cast is here to help us *make life come alive*. You don't have to settle for less. If you wish to solve a problem, develop a skill, heal an emotional trauma, or generate ideas for a creative project, ask for help from the supporting cast members. Guest stars don't need to be *physically* present, which means they can arrive as soon as you invite them. Just be sure to *call in the best*!

✍ *Who are the members of your supporting cast? List them or sketch a picture of yourself surrounded by these guests. You may wish to collect pictures of your supporting cast and create a collage.*

Angels delight in setting stages, turning on spotlights, and making Stars out of bit players like me.
LILY CAVELL

Touring the Set

The Setting and Backdrop

Inside your mind, in addition to the people, there are *places*. The inner theatre setting represents the entire backdrop of consciousness—the *context* of all your life's activities. Just as stars need a night sky in which to sparkle, inner stars need a theatre in which to perform.

To explore the depths and heights of yourself, you can imagine places and spaces inside, thereby creating a structure for your consciousness. This will help you find your way around the nooks and crannies of your mind.

In touring the set, you'll explore inner dimensions and realms that are generally uninvestigated. You'll go to the farther reaches of human consciousness to push the limits of your existing reality. Sound far-out? It is! And also *far in*.

Yes, the play takes place in infinite inner space. It takes place in the eternal *now*.

First of all, to get oriented, you may wish to examine the theatre environment. I like to imagine that the back of my theatre opens onto a beautiful walking garden, which I call the Garden of Great Expectations. Being in nature is vital to my health and happiness, so I've created this botanical garden that leads to a quiet lake. At the edge of the lake is a small amphitheater I use on summer afternoons and evenings. These are some of my images. Your theatre may have an entirely different setting.

After exploring the outside, you'll enter the theatre and investigate the auditorium and stage, the shadowy basement, and the mysterious upstairs. Then you'll locate your director's inner sanctum—a very important place inside your mind.

So, if you are ready, let's begin the tour of your magnificent playhouse.

A man must be arched and buttressed from within, else the temple crumbles to the dust.
MARCUS AURELIUS

The Theatre

You are standing on the corner of Imagination Street and Adventure Avenue. Take a deep breath and look around.

In front of you is your own magnificent theatre. Observe the various aspects of the environment. What is the landscape in front of the theatre? . . . Walk all the way around and explore the sides and the back. What do you discover?

Observe your theatre in this setting. Is it a large and spacious structure, or a small and cozy one? . . . What is the style of the architecture? Of what materials is it made?

What sounds do you hear as you stand outside? . . . What aromas waft your way?

Be aware of your feet on the ground. Listen to the sound of your steps as you walk up the path to the entrance.

Take hold of the door handle. Is it cool or warm to your touch?

Now open the door. . . . Step into the foyer and look around. Is it light, dim, dark? . . . What colors do you notice? . . . What feelings do you have?

Since you are the owner, you can decorate or change anything you desire. If there's anything you'd like to change, just give the command and see it as you'd like it to be.

Now find a comfortable chair in the lounge and sit down. Lean back and relax.

✐ *Sketch, design, or write a description of your theatre and its setting.*

I have made my world and it is a much better world than I ever saw outside.
LOUISE NEVELSON

The Stage

Inside the theatre, doors open to the auditorium, revealing the stage. The stage of your mind is also known as your "field of awareness." It's where your attention is focused *now*. The issues that are up front for you take place on this stage.

At this moment on my own stage, the action takes place inside my adobe casa near Santa Fe, New Mexico. (You'll notice how my inner and outer worlds interconnect.) The spotlight shines on my Writer as I sit at my computer. My desk is cluttered with papers. I hear the whirring sound of my computer but also the intermittent song of a red-winged black bird outside my window. The taste of mint tea lingers in my mouth. Other inner actors are resting. The name of this week's play could be *Writer in Paradise*.

In describing what was taking place on the stage of her life, one enthusiastic workshop participant said, "The name of my current play is *The Clan*. It's all taking place in a glade. About six of my actors are having a picnic, talking about a trip they are going to make this summer. They discuss plans and what they need to do. They are eating and drinking and laughing. They are looking forward to adventure."

"On my stage," a male participant stated, "my actors are arguing about the best approach to a medical problem I'm having. The drama's called *The Pros and Cons of Allopathic and Naturopathic Medicine*."

And a woman in her mid-fifties shared, "The issue that's in the spotlight for me is how to juggle the needs of my aging mother with the needs of my family. My actors are angry with me for not making some important decisions about a nursing home for Mom. The name of this melodrama could be either *Sitting on the Fence* or *Caught in the Middle*."

In this moment, in your play, everything you see, taste, smell, hear, touch, or intuit is on stage in your awareness. When you are aware of something, it is "in the spotlight." When something or someone is "in the light," it or they can be seen and known. By focusing on your immediate experience, you can become aware of the action on stage. What's currently in the spotlight of your life?

On the stage it's always now; the personages are standing on that razor-edge between the past and the future, which is the essential character of conscious being.
THORNTON WILDER

Basically, everywhere you stand is the center of the world. You're always standing in the middle of sacred space.
BLACK ELK

What's on Stage?

Back in the foyer of your inner theatre, notice the open doors to the auditorium and walk through. For a moment, stand in the aisle and observe the seats . . . and the stage with the curtains drawn. What are the designs and colors of this place?

Everyone who walks up to you has entered your stage and it's no accident. There is a purpose.
PEMA CHÖDRÖN

Walk slowly to the front and slip into a seat. Look toward the stage and observe how the draperies flow gracefully onto the floor. Note their color, texture, and weight.

Now sit back and relax. Something is about to happen. . . . The lights dim and the orchestra begins to play a prelude. What do you hear?

Slowly the curtains open . . . revealing an ordinary scene from your present life-situation. What is the setting? . . . What are the props— furniture, equipment, and objects?

In the spotlight, one of your inner actors is performing. Who is this lead character? . . . What is it doing? . . . How is it dressed?

Now another inner actor steps forward. Who is this character and what role is it playing? . . . How do the two characters relate to each other?

Are other actors present? Is one of the actors suffering? . . . If so, which part does it play? Where is this character in the scene?

Is the performance like a comedy, soap opera, farce, or melodrama? Is it a mystery play, morality play, passion play, charade, giveaway show, magic act, or tragedy? In what ways? What might be the name of your play?

✍ Take time to write briefly about your play, then sketch the scene on paper.

The Backstage

What goes on behind the scenes? What takes place backstage in your consciousness?

Symbolically the backstage area is your *preconscious*. This is information or data within range of consciousness, but not yet perceived. It is the information you hold in the *back of your mind*. In his book *What Freud Really Said*, David Stafford-Clark stated, "Consciousness is the spotlight which, sweeping the arena, lights up just that area on which it falls. Everything outside its illumination, but within its range, is preconsciousness."

Assagioli called this dimension the *middle unconscious* in his book *Psychosynthesis*. He explained that "in this inner region, our various experiences are assimilated, our ordinary mental and imaginative activities are elaborated and developed in a sort of psychological gestation before their birth into the light of consciousness." In other words, preconscious content can be something we knew before or something we are about to discover.

For example, when you wake from a dream but can't remember what it was, or when you can't recall the name of a person who was just introduced to you, that information has just slipped behind the curtains of your awareness. On the other hand, when you have a sense of something that is about to happen, or when you are searching for the right words to say, that information is just ready to slip onto the stage of your awareness.

If you want to bring something from behind the curtains into the spotlight of consciousness, you can call it forth through active recall, free association, dreams, guided imagery, symbolic projection, forms of hypnosis, and receptive and creative meditation. For example, in the exercise *What's on Stage?*, you allowed spontaneous images to come to you from "somewhere." From where do you think they came? They slipped from your preconscious onto the stage

When actors leave the stage after playing their parts, they return to their dressing rooms backstage. Although they are *out of sight,* they are not *out of mind.* They live their continuous life unobserved, behind the scenes, but most will return to the stage another time, another day.

Conscious strainings are letting loose subconscious allies behind the scenes.
WILLIAM JAMES

Backstage and to the left (from the audience's perspective) you will find a door leading downstairs to the basement. To the right, you'll find another door leading upstairs to the mysterium. In the upper rooms, ideas and images gestate before their birth into consciousness. And as the poet Rainer Maria Rilke said: "You must give birth to your images. They are the future waiting to be born."

In the inner theatre, a lot goes on behind the scenes. Fortunately, you can relax and feel assured that things are being taken care of properly without your having to pay attention to all the details! You can depend on the wisdom of your backstage crew, who work tirelessly without recognition.

The Basement

The basement of your mind! Can you imagine what's in the lower rooms of your theatre?

The basement represents your *subconscious* mind, or the *lower unconscious* region. To go downstairs may seem a bit like descending into a dark, dank cellar or into an abyss. You may even feel a bit reluctant to discover what's there.

Why go to the basement? We go to this lower level to discover what is obscure and unknown in our psyche. We go to discover the depths of our being. We go so we, as directors, can have a better knowledge of what's going on in the theatre. Can you imagine a director not knowing what's in the rooms below the stage?

To enter the basement, switch on a light and descend the stairs. Down here, what you'll find is stuff from the past. In fact, your whole ancestral history is stored in the stacks and archives. Your amazing mind has recorded and continues to record pictures, sounds, smells, tastes, and sensations from every moment of your day's performance. Every tiny detail is noted and stored in your memory banks.

Dusting things off and browsing around, you'll find old scrapbooks, treasure chests, a media center, and, most impressively, a state-of-the-art *Innernet*. On the Innernet, information is sent by and received from every member of the entourage. Yes, everyone in the inner theatre is in constant contact. What's more, the operation of this sophisticated communications network takes place completely off stage, outside of your awareness.

On the Innernet, your daily dramas are sorted and stored in files. If the day's drama goes well and the plot is resolved, the information is placed in the category of "Completed Plays." Your actors derive a deep sense of goodness and confidence when an issue is resolved in your life. However, if your day's performance is not resolved or completed, the information is filed in the category of "Incomplete Plays." Actors involved in an unfinished drama keep reminding you that something isn't right. They sneak back on stage and interrupt other parts of your life because they want to rework their mistakes and resolve their conflict. They want to feel successful.

. . . each one of us possesses a heritage within us—a heritage to which generations and centuries of achievement and calamity, of triumph and failure, have contributed.
CARDINAL KAROL WOJTYLA (LATER POPE JOHN PAUL II)

If you manage to live divinely—even for one second—eternity is in that second, and a recording exists which will live on forever.
OMRAAM M. AÏVANHOV

Unfinished plays linger in the back of your mind and carry a negative charge. You may feel frustrated, confused, or anxious. You may get a headache, feel impatient, or blame others for the way you feel. Inevitably, if you don't solve the mystery, your actors will reenact the same theme over and over with other people until they get it right. (Frequently, if your actors are in turmoil when you go to sleep, they will try to complete the drama in the "Dream Theatre.")

Fortunately, you can resolve old conflicts. You can heal unpleasant memories of the past. *How?* You do this by taking the old script, going back to the problem section, and rewriting a new script the way you want it to be! You aren't limited by time or space. You can change the past in the theatre of your mind!

Here's an example of what I'm talking about. In a workshop I was leading, John, a thirtysomething Frenchman, told about a painful memory that lingered vividly in his mind for years. He said: "I was seven years old and living in a small town outside Paris. Our school was preparing for a class coronation. The teachers were bestowing crowns on all the students and we all lined up to receive our crowns. I was the last one in line, and when the teacher got to me, there weren't any left. She was short one crown."

Visibly distressed with the memory, John continued: "The worst thing was that no one paid any attention to me. The teacher looked the other way and ignored my presence. I was deeply hurt and felt a strong sense of rejection. I thought that I had no value. After school, I walked home, sobbing all the way."

As John told his story, our hearts ached for the little seven-year-old and for the adult man who was reliving the memory. At the coffee break, several members of the class took poster board, oil pastels, glue, and glitter and created a magnificent crown. Then in private, it was passed to every member of the group to autograph on the inside.

When the break was over, we declared that we were going to have a new coronation in honor of John. Behold! The new, beautiful crown was presented to John—our designated leading man. As we all marched around, we told him that he was, indeed, a royal person, and that we honored, respected, and recognized his princely self. With the step of a highborn, and with tears streaming down his cheeks, John marched with us, wearing the crown and accepting our accolades.

That day, John's Incomplete Play was transferred to the section for Completed Plays. Recently I spoke to John over the phone and he said that his now ten-year-old crown was within reach as we spoke. He even read aloud the names on the inside and stated emphatically, "This is something I will take to my grave! It means a lot to me."

We can always create new endings for bad memories, because the inner world is fluid and dynamic. And physiologically we respond the same way to images as we do to actual situations. Changing unresolved dramas affects all of our future performances.

Fortunately, the basement isn't just filled with cobwebs, monsters, and old Horror Shows, it also holds all the beauty, love, and peak experiences of our lifetime. All of our great memories are stored here as well. These memories nourish us. They sustain us when times are tough. I love remembering the hour my son learned to walk. The expression on his face and the excitement that filled our home are memories that I shall always cherish.

Now that you've had a glimpse of the basement, it might be the time to organize your cleaning crew—the parts of you who like to organize and make things shine. Get out the brooms and rags and start cleaning up! Sweep out the cobwebs. Open the windows to get fresh air. Look behind doors that have been locked for a long time. And play upbeat music to make the work more fun.

Are you reluctant to do this? Some people are concerned that if they clean their basement, life will become boring. But boredom is not the opposite of chaos! If you clean your basement, you won't give up *excitement*, you'll give up *tension*. You'll feel lighter and you'll have more time to create what you want. Can you imagine what it would feel like to have a clean basement? Can you imagine the peace of mind—the relief?

✍ If you explored your basement, what would you encounter: Musty smells? . . . locked doors? . . . muffled voices? If you switched on the lights and began to clean the main areas, what would you do first? What feelings arise when you consider cleaning the basement?

If you unlock a door for the first time, open it cautiously. Only enter when you are comfortable with the open door.
FLEMMING FUNCH

If a door won't open, you must save it for a later attempt.
FLEMMING FUNCH

The Mysterium

The inner theatre not only has a basement, but it also has an upstairs and a sunroof. This light, lofty region can be called the *mysterium* of your mind. While the basement is your subconscious, the mysterium is the *superconscious*, or *higher unconscious*. It's called the mysterium because you can never, in all your years, discover everything it holds.

This upstairs is a vast region beyond your ordinary awareness and comprehension. It is dynamic, ever-changing, and ever-expanding. It is the source of your higher feelings of compassion, love, and ecstasy. It is the realm of pure light and celestial music.

Because of the pure atmosphere in the mysterium, disharmony and evil cannot enter. You won't find your actors fighting up here. The conditions simply do not allow it. French philosopher and spiritual master Omraam Aïvanhov noted: "When we rise to the higher levels, the beings of the lower levels cannot follow us because above a certain altitude they cannot breathe."

The mysterium, being beyond time and space, is the eternal *now*. It opens to the field of all possibilities and, therefore, attracts all possible combinations of ideas, putting them together to generate inspiration, intuition, and creativity. It is magical, in that it manifests whatever you think, imagine, and desire. It is beautiful and peaceful. Nothing can destroy it.

When you go upstairs, you can find your Genie—the genius part of yourself. You can also find your inner Magician and your Wise Old Man and Woman. You can find the Mommy and Daddy you've always wanted. You can even find the Lover you've been waiting for.

In contrast to the basement, which holds the patterns of *what you have been* in this lifetime, the upstairs holds all the information about your existence prior to your birth as well as the magnificent blueprint for *what you may be*. Think about this! The mysterium holds the perfected pattern for what every inner actor can become. It's truly a treasure house of wisdom and spiritual possibilities that can enrich us as we gain access to it.

When you visit the mysterium, you can travel *forward* in time, create the future, and bring it back into the present, where you can

The soul has a private door into divinity . . .
ST. AUGUSTINE

You can be pulled forward by the future rather than held back by the past.
LAZARIS

manifest it in time and space. In other words, you can dream of castles in the sky, then come back and build foundations under them.

Albert Einstein once said, "The most beautiful thing we can experience is the mysterious. It is the source of all true science." I would add that it is also the source of all true religion and education and medicine and politics and entertainment and therapy and business! Well, maybe all of life!

To explore this place of mystery, climb the stair steps to the higher regions of your mind. Take hold of the staircase. Make the ascent. In *A Home for the Soul*, architect Anthony Lawlor explains that "a staircase creates a vertical bridge for the passage of consciousness from one plane of experience to another." So leave the stage, where your daily routine takes place, and explore the mysterium.

The mystery never fails to nourish and heal me.
JOHN CARMODY

Visiting the Mysterium

Sit back, relax, and prepare to visit your inner theatre mysterium.

Imagine that your stage is now empty and quiet. The audience is gone, the bits of trash have been picked up, the seats and aisles have been cleaned. All is in order.

Step onto the stage and walk behind the curtain to the right side. In this right wing, notice an exquisite staircase leading upward. Light streams from above.

As you begin to climb the stairs, notice large, golden mirrors on both sides, reflecting your image. Take a moment to observe how the lighting outlines your body and brings out the best in you. . . . You feel radiant and attractive!

As you reach the top of the stairs, take a moment to allow your eyes to adjust to the light streaming from the skylight. . . . Everything is illuminated.

Step forward and, as you approach the dazzling wall in front of you, notice that it seems to disappear. Hmm . . . you realize that the walls are illusions. You can reach out and touch the clouds. In fact, you can even step lightly onto the clouds and walk about.

. . . experience of the superconscious reality cancels out fear . . .
ROBERTO ASSAGIOLI

I am going out into the universe to stroll on the Milky Way. . .
HUGH ROBERT ORR

With our thoughts we create the world.
BUDDHA

May the Great Mystery make sunrise in your heart.
SIOUX INDIAN

With amazement, you walk carefully until you gain more confidence. Giving yourself permission to do so, you begin to roll and tumble and dance. You sense that you can even fly.

This mysterious place defies your comprehension. The space goes on forever. With clear, inner vision, you notice the scintillating light particles in the clouds—similar to the ribbons of the northern lights. These are the light-waves from which all things are made. From these waves, you can create whatever you wish by mixing and matching any combination of ideas and images.

This is where you experience the magic of creation. You influence what occurs in your life by thinking about what you really want and establishing a clear picture—like a three-dimensional hologram. Your feelings and desires add color and power to the thought-forms.

Here, there are no "ground rules." Everything is possible. You can think, build, and create. Light-waves of thought, images, and desires come together to form particles of matter. From this alive field of energy and information, you can materialize what you want.

Find a comfortable place to sit in this mysterium—perhaps on a soft cushion or a cloud. You don't have to do anything at this time. Simply sit quietly in this field of all possibilities—and just be!

You can trust that something good is happening even though you can't see how it's all working out. Simply know that life is divinely guided. Surrender to the mystery!

In time, when you're ready to leave the mysterium, return to the staircase and descend the steps slowly. . . . Notice your luminous reflection in the golden mirrors. . . . Re-enter the auditorium and walk down the aisle and out through the door of your inner theatre. . . . Walk back to the room where you are presently sitting and feel the weight of your body on the chair. Breathe deeply and stretch.

✍ *Reflect on your experience in the mysterium. Sketch pictures of what happened, allowing your superconscious mind to do the drawing.*

The Director's Inner Sanctum

There's a place in the inner theatre designed specifically for you—the director. This place is the director's inner sanctum, a private, sacred space where you go to gain equilibrium, or to relax and just be yourself. You are in this place in consciousness when you feel most at home. In fact, since you carry your inner sanctuary inside, you can never leave home without it!

Anthony Lawlor must have been describing this special place when he said, "Places conducive to solitude are stable and orderly. Sounds are muted and draw the mind to quietness. Textures are soft and smooth. Light and colors are quiet and harmonious. Fragrances are soothing and fresh." What a beautiful description of an environment that calms and nourishes one's spirit!

A Swiss woman attending a workshop of mine discovered through imagery that her inner sanctuary was filled with music and with yellow-white light. She told us: "The light surrounds me and I hear silence *and* music. I hear sounds that are outside the spectrum of sound, but can be felt as vibrations in my body. I am able to hear the sounds of the universe, both far and near." She went on to describe seeing an abundance of fresh, natural foods and clear, cool water. "This place has exactly what I want when I want it, and I am totally supported in being an effective leader of my cast of characters."

Sixteenth-century French essayist Michel de Montaigne knew the importance of creating privacy and taking time for reflection. He wrote: "We must reserve a back shop, wholly our own, entirely free, wherein to establish our true liberty and our principal retreat and solitude . . . there to talk and laugh as if without wife, without children, without possessions, without followers. . . . Retire into yourself, but first prepare to receive yourself there."

In a *Good Housekeeping* interview, television show hostess Joan Lunden spoke of the importance of the inner refuge she created for herself at home. She said she was intimidated at first by the thought of spending time alone there, but the more she used her quiet space, the more rewards she gained—rewards such as calmness and optimism. She explained that her new calmness gives her a voice to better communicate with others, which she does superbly.

Home is where the heart is not famished, the eye not starved, the Sacred not banished or desecrated.
FREDERICK FRANCK

Within you there is a stillness and sanctuary to which you can retreat at any time and be yourself.
HERMANN HESSE

Within each of us there is a sacred emptiness. The quality of that space is love, kindness, and mercy.
STEPHEN LEVINE

We can also take the advice of Omraam Aïvanhov, who said, "As often as possible, try to create an inner zone of silence, harmony, and light. These are the conditions your spirit needs if it is to expand, to soar . . ."

In the following exercise, prepare to receive yourself by finding the sanctum your spirit needs to expand and soar.

A Room with a View

Using your creative imagination, find the inner sanctum that belongs to your director-self. Where in your inner theatre is it located? . . . Notice the setting and environment. . . . What is the climate?

What is the size and shape of your sacred space? . . . What is the view from this location?

Notice the colors and the lighting, which are just right for you. What hues do you find to be quiet and harmonious? . . . Notice the architectural features . . . the textures . . . the order. Does it have furnishings or is it empty of things?

Do you hear sounds or is it quiet? . . . Are there fragrances?

Consciously create this sacred space so you can feel peaceful and at home.

If you listen carefully you will hear the sound of silence in all sounds.
GWEN HARRISON

✍ *You may wish to make a collage of pictures and words that capture the essence of your inner sanctum or to compose a song or write a poem describing this space. Having established a quiet place inside, begin to find ways to replicate this inner experience in your outer world. Nourish yourself by creating a physical place to call your own.*

The Global Theatre

The same features we discover in our inner theatre are reflected in the Global Theatre on a worldwide scale. Let's take a closer look at this larger setting.

GLOBAL BACKDROP: The Backdrop is the *collective consciousness* of all the actors on the World Stage. This consciousness is more or less the same everywhere in all individuals. For example, we all have a similar understanding of the meaning of a zero, a flag, a family unit, a tribal chief, or even a drama. We understand these concepts because they are part of the Big Mind we create together.

GLOBAL SPOTLIGHT: In the spotlight of human consciousness, you'll find people and events highlighted in the daily news and beamed by satellite to all corners of Earth. One moment the Global Spotlight may shine on a United Nations conflict with a particular country, and another moment on a terrorist bombing at a border province. The world might watch with concern as the leader of a nation undergoes major surgery or as a city tries to survive a natural disaster.

GLOBAL BASEMENT: In the Global Basement, also called the collective *sub*conscious, you'll find the cosmic memory bank that holds humanity's evolutionary heritage. This includes all the joys and triumphs and all the savagery and tragedies of human beings throughout time. Everything that has been a part of human history is available, on record, in humanity's holographic mind.

GLOBAL MYSTERIUM: In the Global Mysterium, also called the collective *super*conscious, you'll tap into the highest aspirations, ideals, and creative endeavors of humanity. This is the Higher Mind that holds the potential for civilization. Our collective future is pregnant with possibilities. Magnificent Plays for the new millennium are waiting to be performed by us—the world's players.

QUALITIES OF THE
UNIVERSAL FIELD
Fully awake
Total potential
Organizing power
Infinite correlation
Perfect orderliness
Infinite dynamism
Infinite creativity
Pure knowledge
All possibilities
Self-sufficiency
Perfect balance
Infinite silence
Harmonizing
Evolutionary
Unbounded
Nourishing
Unmanifest
Integrating
Simplicity
Invincible
Immortal
Purifying
Freedom
Bliss
DEEPAK CHOPRA
CREATING AFFLUENCE

Claiming

the

Director's

Chair

The Director's Chair

To produce a successful play (perhaps even a divine comedy), it's necessary to claim your director's chair, become acquainted with your players and playwright, and discover the secrets of directing.

Somewhere in your inner theatre you'll find your director's chair. This chair represents your position of inner authority. It serves as a reminder that *you* are responsible for your personal performance.

If you haven't been using your chair, you need to discover where it is. Perhaps it has been in storage, or one of your actors might be using it. Some people even realize that they have given their chair away to someone else, or that someone has taken it from them.

Claiming Your Director's Chair

Return to your inner sanctum and search for your director's chair. You may find it in a clear, open space—or it might be where you haven't seen it in a long time. It might even be in storage.

When you find it, examine it closely. . . . What does your chair look like? What condition is it in? Is it comfortable? Is it the right size and shape for you? Do the materials, colors, and textures reflect your center of inner authority? Is it elaborate or simple? Does it have special magical features?

Determine if this is a suitable chair for you. . . . If it isn't, design a new one. Remember, it is your chair. You are the one in charge. You can make any changes that you desire.

Since this is your personal chair, be sure to put your name on it.

Affirm: "I claim my director's chair and accept my position of inner authority."

✍ *Jot down your insights and sketch a picture of your chair.*

My director's chair is magic. If anyone tries to sit in my chair, the seat falls out!
DAVID KING
11 YEARS OLD

Impostor Director

Prior to the time that we develop awareness of ourselves as director, our dramas just seem to "happen." Someone in the troupe takes charge. Sometimes an inner Parent assumes leadership and tells the cast what to do. Sometimes the Skeptic, the Slave Driver, the Victim, or the Dominator occupies the director's chair.

Often one of the strong actors believes *it* is the director. This actor—an imposter—may run the show for a long time, demanding that other actors see and do things its way. The problem is this: the impostor lacks objectivity and sees situations only from a limited point of view. The imposter becomes invested in making a particular impression on others and punishes cast members who question its authority. When we demonstrate egotism, become invested in appearances, and wield power over others, we can be certain that an impostor has taken over!

Imagine the impostor's surprise when you—the *real* director—claim your chair. Is the impersonator going to step down and compliantly give up its power? No way! There's certain to be a battle as that strong actor fights to maintain control. Once you realize that *you* are the director and that *you* are in charge of your entourage, you will definitely have to deal with the impostor. This actor, who thought it was the director, must give up the leader's chair. Releasing attachment to a long-held position and a corresponding self-image is not easy, but it must be done. This process inevitably creates conflict—an inevitable by-product of our development. It is an inner war we are certain to experience as we evolve.

In making this change of leadership, your intent is not to destroy the strong actor, but to redefine its duties and give it a new role *under your supervision*. Acceptance, not murder, is your solution. You may even be so kind as to give the former imposter a chair marked "Director's Assistant."

Inner actors are not the only ones who try to take over your life. You may find a parent, a partner, a boss, a religious leader, or another powerful person sitting in your director's chair. It's possible that you have even *offered* your chair to others. Essentially you may have said: *"Here, take my chair. Tell me what to do."*

Someone's been sitting in my chair!
GOLDILOCKS
THE THREE BEARS

When I allow someone to sit in my chair, I feel like a puppet in a puppet theatre.
GISELA HOFMANN

Eventually, though, we discover that this doesn't work in the long run. Something deep inside pulls us toward *self-mastery*. Ultimately, we are responsible for our own lives and how we choose to live.

✍ *Do you have an actor who thinks it is the director? As director, thank this actor for taking charge while you have been away, then announce to the cast that you are assuming your rightful place. Now take another look: do others also sit in your director's chair sometimes? As director, give these people the honor of becoming members of your supporting cast, not authorities of your life. Your director's chair belongs only to you!*

Director's Identity

Who are you as the leader of your inner theatre? Are you a director simply because you call yourself a director? Does sitting in a director's chair actually make you a director?

To develop inner authority and gain mastery in your theatre, you need to know two secrets: 1) *who you are* and 2) *what you do*. Let's look at the first. What *is* the secret of your identity?

More than Roles

In the experience you had earlier with three actors and the director, you discovered that *you are more than your parts.* Until we experience who we are behind our masks, we believe we *are* the role we happen to be playing in the moment. We lose sight of the larger performance and limit our expression to the repertoire of the actor who's in the spotlight.

By over-identifying with a particular actor, we limit our understanding of who we are. Then, when that role changes, our sense of self also changes. For example, if a woman finds her identity in her husband and then loses him through death or divorce, does she lose herself because she no longer plays the role of a wife? If a man fails in a business venture, does he lose himself because he no longer plays a CEO role?

Who you are does *not* depend on your roles, situations, or costumes. As director, you are the one behind all your masks. Roberto Assagioli often stated, "We are dominated by everything with which we are identified, and we have dominion over everything from which we disidentify."

We are dominated by everything with which we are identified, and we have dominion over everything from which we disidentify.
ROBERTO ASSAGIOLI

More than Body, Emotions, Mind

Confusing who you are with the roles you play is common, but it is just as common to confuse your self with your body ("I am tired"), your emotions ("I am depressed"), your mind ("I am forgetful"), or your beliefs ("My church is the right church"). While you may *have* a tired body, depressed feelings, a fallible memory, or seemingly true beliefs, *you* are more.

As you sit in your director's chair, experience the following reality as your core identity. This awareness can radically change your life if you are intent on discovering the deeper truth of your beingness.

Who Am I as Director?

*To begin, pay special attention to your **body**. How are you sitting? What is the taste in your mouth? Where is the tension in your body?*

Your body—the most physical expression of who you are—is your way of getting around in the world. Your body is always changing, moving, and growing older. You continually shift from being physically active to being inactive; from being under the weather to being healthy and energetic.

Who is aware of your physical condition? Who takes care of your body? Who chooses, decides on, and initiates action? Who is the "you" that is more than your body?

*In addition to having a body, you also have **feelings** and **emotions** that add color to your life. Emotions are like waves of the ocean; they ebb and flow. When a wave wells up in you, it may momentarily jostle or submerge you, but then it crests and recedes, usually within seconds or minutes.*

One thing is certain: feelings and emotions are always changing. Sometimes your feelings are positive and sometimes negative. Sometimes you express emotions freely, at other times you control or suppress them.

Who watches your emotions ebb and flow? Who modulates or changes their flow and direction? Who registers feelings? Who is the "you" that is more than your feelings?

*In addition to having a body and emotions, you are also a being with **intelligence**. Your intellect is your means of discovery and expression in the world. You use your mind to think, plan, conceptualize, and fantasize. Often you change your mind, focus your thinking, or censor your thoughts.*

The body is a sacred garment. It's your first and last garment; it is what you enter life in and what you depart life with, and it should be treated with honor.
MARTHA GRAHAM

My body is not who I am.
CHRISTOPHER REEVE

But you must not follow your feelings. Your feelings must follow you.
ROBERTO ASSAGIOLI

Thoughts and ideas are like clouds in the sky. They accumulate and dissipate. Like the sky, your mind is sometimes light and clear, and sometimes it is filled with darkness and turbulence.

Who observes your thoughts, beliefs, memories, and ideas? Who is aware of all this? Who thinks? Who gives direction to your mental activities? Who is the "you" that is more than your mind?

Yes, who is the "you" that thinks, feels, and acts? Would you agree that you are more than these? If so, experiment with the following statements:

I am my mind, yet I am more.
I am my emotions, yet I am more.
I am my body, yet I am more.

Then who is the "I" that is more? Try out the following claims:

Since I observe, I know I am a center of awareness.
Since I feel and care, I know I am a center of love.
Since I choose and act, I know I am a center of will.

Essentially, I am a center of awareness, love, and will.
I am the one behind all my masks.
I am my self!

You can always step back from a role you play. You can step back and observe a thought or idea swirling around in your mind. You can even step back from the perpetual currents of feelings that arise within you and look at them objectively. But what you can never move away from is your self. The self is who you are when you can't step back any farther.

The more fully you realize and accept who you truly are, the more easily you will be able to walk with dignity and poise. As director, you'll be prepared to take charge of your life.

The Unchanging Self

As director, affirm the following statements:

While the conditions, age, and circumstances of my life are ever-changing, my self remains steady, ageless, and indestructible.

Although my body changes as I grow older, my self does not grow old.

Although my body becomes tired or ill, my self does not become tired or ill.

Although my feelings and moods ebb and flow, my self does not ebb and flow.

Although my states of consciousness are ever-changing, my self does not waver.

Although my roles change, my self does not vary.

I—my self—remain stable in the midst of all change.

Director's Tasks

To develop inner authority and gain mastery in your theatre, you need not only to know who you are, but also *what you do*. Now that you have experienced a deeper awareness of your director's identity, let's take a look at the second secret.

In the same way that a theatre troupe doesn't just happen to be successful, the parts of one's personality don't just happen to be harmonious. Only a trained director can orchestrate the cast and create a smoothly operating production. The director is responsible for pulling the show together.

There are simple principles of integration that can be mastered. While attaining this mastery may sound *complex,* it doesn't have to be *complicated.*

Remember when you first learned to drive a car? In the beginning everything seemed so complicated and potentially dangerous. Yet in spite of your fears, you sat in the driver's seat and became aware of the essential mechanics. Gaining confidence, you discovered that maneuvering the big wheeled machine wasn't so hard after all. And now when you drive, you don't even think of what you're doing. It just comes naturally.

Driving a car and directing your life are similar experiences. Both take conscious effort in the beginning to learn the principles and mechanics. Once you learn, you feel confident and independent. In both, you need to remain alert and aware of all the conditions, which are constantly changing.

The way to do is to be.
LAO TZU, CHINESE SAGE

You already have what you need to become the director. Who you *are* forms the foundation for what you *do*. This is the relationship between *being* and *doing*, or between *isness* and *business*.

The secret of *who* you are (your identity) holds the secret to what you *do* (your task). As director, your task is threefold:

1. As a center of awareness, to *recognize* your actors.
2. As a center of love, to *accept* your actors.
3. As a center of will, to *empower* your actors.

You may wonder what ultimately happens when you carry out these three steps in directing. Everything happens!

When you open your *mind* and *recognize* your actors,
you develop self-*awareness*.
When you open your *heart* and *accept* your actors,
you develop self-*love*.
When you activate your *will* and *empower* the cast,
you develop self-*mastery*.

Here you can see the director's task so clearly that it seems unbelievably simple. And yet, the whole directing process depends on this understanding. Truth is revealed in simplicity, so let me say it one more time in a slightly different way:

I have → a mind, heart, and body.
I am → a center of awareness, love, and will.
I do → recognize, accept, and empower my actors.

As you'll discover, the secret to successful directing depends on the way you use your intelligence, love, and will. These three characteristics are inextricably bound together, generating the power for your play on Earth. In *An Actor Prepares*, Constantin Stanislavski expressed it this way: "The power of these motive forces is enhanced by their interaction. They support and incite one another with the result that they always act at the same time and in close relationship. When we call our mind into action, by the same token we stir our will and feelings. It is only when these forces are cooperating harmoniously that we can create freely."

When your head, heart, and body work together (yes, it happens sometimes), you experience *synergy*—energies flowing together, each enhancing the other, making spontaneity and creativity so much easier!

You'll notice that your accomplished *star players* already have an admirable blend of these three forces. They use their intelligence, they care about others, and they act with strength and courage. For example, if you're a good parent, your inner Parent will 1) see and understand your Child, 2) show love and compassion, and 3) support the child's emerging will. Or, if you're a successful investor, your inner Investor

You should look at life unmasked, in the mirror of your experiences. . . . Look at the perpetual current of emotions and thoughts that arise within you. Go into the heart of our aspirations, dreams, hopes, and despairs. Dive deep into the mute cravings of your inner self. Life is manifesting itself through all these channels and demanding that you seek understanding with your highest intelligence, wisdom, love, and vision.
PARAMAHANSA
YOGANANDA

will 1) study options and make wise decisions, 2) choose investments with humanitarian values, and 3) take appropriate action.

On the other hand, your *unaccomplished actors* have not *yet* learned how to express their intelligence, love, and will in a constructive or balanced way. For example, the dour inner Critic uses the power of its sharp intellect to cut others down, without showing any empathy or compassion. The inner Slave Driver demands immediate action from others without showing any concern for their feelings. The inner Martyr has great empathy, but doesn't know how to serve others without suffering and making others feel guilty for being served.

To become *accomplished,* the Critic must develop *heart,* at which point it will no longer be able to maintain an accusing attitude and, by contrast, will become a discerning Analyst. The Slave Driver must develop *understanding* and *empathy* before he'll become an effective Manager. The Martyr must develop *wisdom* and *will* before she'll care equally for herself and give without attaching strings.

As Deepak Chopra stated: ". . . we are divinity in disguise, and the gods and goddesses in embryo that are contained within us seek to be fully materialized." To develop their divine potential, actors need the understanding, love, and strength of their director.

Robert's Story

To demonstrate how one director assisted an actor in developing its star quality, I'd like to tell you the story of Robert, a distinguished, fifty-year-old Los Angeles businessman. For fifteen years, Robert was intensely involved in entertainment research and consulting and in developing products that included toys and games for children. He did his job well but wasn't really enjoying life. Something was missing and he had a nagging urge to free himself from what he described as a "contrived type of energy." He told me, "In my life, I've learned that work and fun are incompatible. I keep thinking that I must work hard. I *pump up* on a daily basis in order to work effectively and to be a success. A concomitant part of working and being a success is being smart and serious."

I asked Robert to step back from his smart, serious, Businessman-actor and take his director's chair. From there he observed the Businessman's contrived energy.

. . . once the relevant lesson has been learned, the cause of suffering disappears.
ROBERT ASSAGIOLI

I asked him when he started being that way? From whom did he learn this script? In his imagination, Robert rewound the video of his past performance and observed a critical incident that occurred when he was a boy. It happened one afternoon when little Bobby was helping his father pour a concrete patio in their backyard. Bobby was the gofer for his father and, as such, was expected to pay attention.

Growing tired of waiting for the next order, Bobby began to entertain himself with some nearby boards and tools. He became absorbed in play and didn't hear his father's next call. Angry that Bobby was not paying attention, the man let loose a volley of accusations and belittling remarks. They hit their mark! Bobby "got it." He got the tattered and worn script his father passed on to him that said: *Life is about working, not playing. Playing is a waste of time.*

That day, playful Bobby was pushed off-stage, and serious, Businessman Bob was born. Forty years later, struggling through a midlife crisis, Robert realized that Businessman Bob was soberly designing toys for children, but never was, himself, playing. He was creating magic for others while he forgot about his own little Bobby in the backyard.

With deep feeling, Businessman Bob returned to the scene in his imagination and took little Bobby into his arms. He knew and understood all the feelings the little boy was feeling—and he deeply cared about them.

To change the performance, Business Bob became an advocate for little Bobby and created a new script that said: *Play is important to the human spirit.* He told the little boy that playing was perfectly all right for him and asked if he would like to join in building something together. Delighted, little Bobby handed big Bob a hammer and the two spent the afternoon having fun. Businessman Bob realized that little Bobby was teaching *him* how to lighten up.

Soon after, Robert dissolved his corporate partnership and developed a new enterprise called *The Center for Innertainment.* In this new venture, Robert is able to evoke the best talents of both his Businessman *and* his inner Child. Today, Dr. Robert Reiher is creating an important, creative, and powerful vehicle for personal and social transformation. He is also a great supporter of and a major consultant in my work with the Inner Theatre. His story, along with many others,

To thine own self be true.
SHAKESPEARE

convinces me that fine-tuning our act can give us a new, focused energy for living, which benefits the world as well.

As directors, we can bring home those actors we have sent away, free those we have imprisoned, and honor those we have ignored. Our actors want to become stars someday. They want to develop their intelligence, love, and will. They have something important to contribute and our *privilege* is to be able to discover the gift each has to give. In doing this, we will suffer less and enjoy life more.

✍ *Imagine bringing intelligence, love, and will into balance in your life. What is it like to know you already have wisdom, compassion, and courage?*

Playwright's Partnership

Now that you have claimed your director's chair and have discovered who you are and what you do, it is time to gather high-level support for yourself.

As director, where do you go for this support? Whom do you turn to for inspiration, empathy, and empowerment?

You don't have to direct the show all by yourself! In fact, you'll do best when you don't try to. The most successful, original productions occur when the director communicates with the playwright. Understanding the deeper intentions of the scriptwriter is always helpful in interpreting a play.

Before calling your actors to the stage for an initial meeting, shift your attention toward your playwright—your soul—to receive inspiration and guidance for the tasks ahead. Just as the director gives acknowledgment, love, and support to the actors, the playwright transmits information, unconditional love, and infinite power to the director.

By stepping back, taking a deep breath, and allowing yourself to receive from the playwright, you discover the meaning of being a giver *and* a receiver. When you receive from the playwright, you can give more to your actors and develop a high-quality production. In such open receptivity, you intuitively perceive the deeper meaning and purpose of the play as the playwright reveals it moment by moment.

In trusting these intuitive moments, we *transcend* everyday awareness and move beyond our usual personal perspectives. In communion with the playwright, we undergo a blending of *individuality* and *universality*. We connect with the universal mind (the field of all possibilities), while keeping both feet on the ground.

The blending of individuality and universality is the hallmark of human excellence, as was demonstrated by people such as Leonardo da Vinci, George Frederick Handel, Maria Montessori, Abraham Maslow, and Florence Nightingale. A contemporary example is visionary Jean Houston, internationally know for her work and research regarding the development of our limitless human potentials. In sharing her research findings, Jean has said, "Indeed, as my studies of highly creative and

Discovering the playwright's intention is the part of the director's work upon which all his other choices depend.
STUART VAUGHAN

productive people confirm, a strong relationship to the Beloved of the soul enhances and sustains their work in the world. The local self . . . is not sufficient."

When people experience the transcendent, they often become leaders in their field. Perceiving what is possible, they blaze trails into new territories. Recognizing the meaning and sacredness of life, they live in the moment. Being nonattached to specific results, they allow the creative process to take them as it will. They do what they do because they are compelled by their soul to do it.

Perhaps you are thinking that these possibilities do not apply to you, since you are just an ordinary person, unable to be *great* and *transcendent*!

To give you some encouragement, I'd like to share a vignette from a manuscript written by my friend Victoria Gamber. Victoria had an encounter with one of the greatest men of the twentieth century. His name: Viktor Frankl. His major work: *Man's Search for Meaning*. She wrote:

> When I first read about Frankl's experiences in the Auschwitz concentration camp, I carried his book with me for months. His work lived in my soul, because he had succeeded in remaining whole and compassionate under the most adverse conditions humans had lived through in this century.
>
> I discovered that Frankl was going to be a visiting professor at my university, so I immediately signed up for his course. He first entered the classroom rather meekly and I saw only a middle-aged, slightly balding, rather short individual. My whole being was shocked by this professor who wrote ordinary diagrams on the board, as did my other professors. This was my hero, and the man was simply a man!
>
> As the semester wore on, I grew increasingly puzzled and upset by how ordinary my hero really was. I sat and fumbled with my notes. What was I missing? I knew I was not really getting the message of Viktor Frankl. Then one day, the message came in clearly. That's it! *An ordinary man making an extraordinary connection can do it!*

We probably will not have the passion for the possible until we experience the motivating power of the relationship with the Beloved [soul].
JEAN HOUSTON

. . . even the tragic and negative aspects of life, such as unavoidable suffering, can be turned into a human achievement by the attitude which a man adopts toward his predicament.
VIKTOR FRANKL

Frankl had made the connection and had walked out of the prison camp with himSelf. When allies liberated Frankl at the end of that conflagration, an entire man walked through the gate. Then I knew that it was the nature of the connection and not the nature of the person that was crucial.

Ordinary people like you and me can live extraordinary lives when we connect with soul and with the deeper meanings of our situations. Of course, as you know, people can and do make valuable contributions in life without any conscious spiritual connection. Many directors come up with their own personal interpretations, produce creative performances, and fulfill their *human potential* without considering the playwright's purpose at all. However, they won't be able to fulfill their *spiritual potential* unless they consciously connect with the Author, or Spirit Force. Shows produced without this crucial connection may stimulate feelings, but they will not change hearts. They may impact the senses, but they will not transform lives. They may be convincing, but they will not be truly powerful.

Establishing Contact

The playwright is not a creation of our imagination. Further, knowing that we are the direct, living reflection of this very real spiritual force allows us to tune in and discover the many ways it—our soul—communicates with us. By consciously connecting with our playwright, we can begin to perceive what our play is all about. We can discover the deeper meaning of all that happens as we see our place in the larger scheme of things.

One practical way you can establish contact is to write a letter to your playwright. (Actually, this is a good way for all members of your entourage to communicate with one another.) In talking with your soul, what would you like to say? Are there things you would like to ask for? Things you would like to know?

Since the playwright isn't merely a psychological phenomenon, something you are inventing, this communication is occurring with a larger dimension of yourSelf. You are hearing and sensing a more subtle aspect of your own being. For example, do you sometimes experience flashes of important insight, quiet moments of deep

The Spiritual "I" is omniscient, it sees into the future and has remarkable powers on which we cannot set a limit.
ROBERTO ASSAGIOLI

understanding, occasions of knowing profoundly without knowing how you know? This is probably your intuition, and *intuition is the playwright speaking to you.* Since the playwright doesn't hand over a paper manuscript that outlines the plot, you must learn to acquire information in other ways—to "intuit" the script and listen to the inner Voice.

When you receive a meaningful symbol in your imagination, from where does the symbol come? Who or what plants it in your mind? When you yearn deeply for something, from where does the yearning originate? Who or what arouses it in your heart?

The playwright communicates to us through our intuition, and also through our thoughts, feelings, dreams, longings, desires, and physical sensations. In fact, our Self finds ways through every possible human experience (positive or negative) to get our attention and relate with us.

Remember: the playwright needs us as much as we need the playwright. Without our physical presence, the soul could not play the masquerade on Earth!

Writing Letters

✍ *Write a letter to your playwright and say whatever comes to your mind. Don't edit or censor your writing. Let your words flow even if they seem senseless.*

Next, take a new sheet of paper and write another letter, this time on the topic: "I need your help on . . ."

After you have written the second letter, extend your awareness and imagine yourself becoming bigger than your body . . . bigger than your emotions . . . bigger than your mind. Take a leap in consciousness and "act as if" you are the playwright of your show—the radiant soul behind all your masks. Be the playwright, receiving the letters. From this expanded dimension of awareness, address a letter to yourself as director (using your name.) As the playwright, what would you say to your director-self?

When you are finished, read all three letters as if you were reading them for the first time.

And anyone who wills can hear the Voice. It is within everyone.
MAHATMA GANDHI

Discerning Inner Voices

How can you be sure the playwright wrote the letter? How can you discern the truth of your inner voices?

The familiar voices of our actors often speak so loudly that they drown out the still, small Voice of our soul. With practice, though, we can learn to quiet the babble and listen to divine inspiration.

Usually we can distinguish the Voice of the playwright from the voices of the actors by the power and clarity of the messages. Unlike other voices, the soul's Voice doesn't criticize, rationalize, or dictate what we must do. In regard to this, Piero Ferrucci states poetically, "Like a vibration mysteriously springing from silence, it [the soul's voice] reaches us with a life and will of its own. It is a categorical imperative: Once we have heard it, we know what we must do."

The playwright's Voice is an inner prompting, and when we disregard the message, we have the nagging feeling that we're making a mistake or not playing our part quite right. We know something is a little off.

Helen, a magazine editor who attended one of my workshops, became aware that one of her actors, not her playwright, had been writing her daily scripts. She named this actor "Lillian," after Lillian Hellman, an American playwright who was controversial, cantankerous, and caustic. After removing the veil from her actor's face, Helen wrote:

> My scriptwriter, Lillian, makes her presence known when I am fearful and when I respond to the fear by needing to control the situation. Lillian takes the fear and writes an entire scenario in my head, which always ends tragically. She's good at creating the worst possible outcomes so that I pull myself away from whatever is threatening me—thereby achieving control. Lillian also scripts the roles of anyone else involved in the plot. When others do not follow her script (which they never do), she rewrites frantically, desperately trying to regain and/or maintain a sense of control. It is when Lillian scripts the roles of others that I get tipped off to the fact that it is Lillian at play in my head, and not my intuition.

Every time you don't follow your inner guidance, you feel a loss of energy, loss of power, a sense of spiritual deadness.
SHAKTI GAWAIN

My playwright, on the other hand, always comes to me with messages and guidance from a place of love and gentleness. My playwright communicates mostly in the form of intuition and is interested in me and in my responses to others. Without exception, every time I have followed my intuition, the outcome is positive; conversely, every time I have followed Lillian, I have had to learn lessons the hard way.

What the inner voice says will not disappoint the hoping soul.
SCHILLER

To determine whether an inner voice or prompting is that of the playwright or of an actor, ask yourself three questions:

1. *Does the message ring true?*
2. *Is it loving and compassionate?*
3. *Does it empower others as well as yourself?*

If you answer "yes" to all three, trust the message. If it doesn't ring true, or if it is critical, uncaring, divisive, or dictatorial, the message probably came from an actor and not the playwright. When this happens, don't argue or judge yourself; simply dismiss the impersonator and ask to speak to the *real* playwright—the playwright who speaks a universal truth.

Directing the Cast

First Step in Directing

AS DIRECTOR, I RECOGNIZE MY ACTORS AND ACKNOWLEDGE WHAT IS.

The lights go on in your inner theatre. The curtain opens. Actors fill the stage, waiting to be recognized and acknowledged. All have something to say. All have something to contribute. Welcome them with applause!

As director, your first step in directing is to become aware of the actors who play parts on your stage. Recognition, or *re-cognition,* means to be cognizant of something you already know. This knowing may be unconscious, but when an actor appears in the spotlight, you remember. You say, "Ah, yes. I know this part of me." Recognizing your actors requires *inner-sight* (in-sight), or intuition. You can "know thyself" or, more aptly, "know thy selves!"

"Back in the autumn I had awakened to a growing darkness and cacophony, as if something in my depths were crying out," writes Sue Kidd in her book *When the Heart Waits.* She was describing the beginning of a midlife crisis. "A whole chorus of orphaned voices seemed to speak for all the unlived parts of me, and they came with a force and dazzle that I couldn't contain."

There they were. Voices demanding to be heard. Actors no longer willing to be denied. Yes, inner characters want to end the game of hiding. They want to be found! They want *you* to take your director's chair and recognize and acknowledge their existence.

To recognize your actors, listen to the things you say and observe your patterns of behavior. This kind of self-observation requires *objectivity.* In other words, you need to be a *fair witness.* Think of yourself as a conscientious scientist who attempts to see what *is* rather than what you *want* to see.

With such an attitude, you can *disidentify* from the dramas that you formerly confused with your true identity. Detached observation allows you to separate yourself as director (the observer) from the actors (the observed), and thus distinguish, in consciousness, the self from the personality. Sitting in your chair and having a little distance from an

THE FIRST STEP INVOLVES:
Consciousness
Recognition
Intelligence
Awareness
Knowing
Intuition
Thought
Wisdom
Insight
Light
Mind

When Intuition moved in, she washed all the windows . . .
J. RUTH GENDLER

In a certain moment in the play, there arises the desire to end the game of hiding, and begin being eternally found.
GANGAJI

*A mind that is stretched to
a new idea never returns
to its original dimension.*
OLIVER WENDELL HOLMES

actor creates an open space from which neutrality can arise. This is the only way to see your self as you truly are.

As a center of pure awareness, you can witness all that arises in your life from moment to moment: sensations in your body, emotions bubbling up, thoughts floating by. As director, you simply allow emotions, desires, and thoughts to arise spontaneously because you know that *you are more.* They cannot hurt you or overcome you. (They may overwhelm you but they can't overcome you.)

When you recognize a specific pattern in your behavior (such as nagging your child, paying your bills late, whining when you don't get your way, or feeling hurt when your spouse goes somewhere without you), step back and observe yourself enacting that pattern—as if this part of you were an actor on stage. Don't try to do anything to change the pattern at this time. Simply observe your behavior *without judging it.* Your actor will be delighted that you're paying attention, and in this open space of awareness, you'll realize—even if gradually at first—that you feel vitally alive to infinite possibilities.

When you judge or criticize yourself, the opposite occurs. Judging means you have to evaluate, classify, analyze, and label whatever is the object of your judgment. This creates a lot of mental commotion. So instead of being in a state of open awareness, you're in a state of mental constriction, closed to new possibilities.

Your inner Judge tells you that you're too old, too weak, too poor, too *something.* You're not good enough, smart enough, brave enough. You're just not *right.* What happens is that this crotchety old Judge plops into your director's chair and takes over.

*Critics are like eunuchs
in a harem; they know
how it's done, they've
seen it done every day,
but they're unable
to do it themselves.*
BRENDAN BEHAN

The Judge and Critic are inner actors who need direction. Instead of judging the Judge or criticizing the Critic, simply shoo them out of your director's chair and send them back on stage where they belong. Observe your Judge and the part of you being judged, or the Critic and the part being criticized. Observe their interactions. How does it feel to judge (or criticize)? How does it feel to be judged (or criticized)? How do those two actors behave? Where did they learn their scripts?

The key here is to become aware that these are *parts* you're playing. You can't depend on them to run your show. Nor would you want them to. As you become aware of your players, you can help them find better ways to act.

Actor's Intelligence

Each inner character has a mind of its own, which means that you have a *multiple intelligence*. Imagine taking the intelligence quotient (IQ) of your inner cast. You'd find some to be at genius level, some average, and some total simpletons. (The inner Judge loves IQ tests because they make easier the job of drawing conclusions about who is better or worse, smarter or dumber. The director, on the other hand, is less concerned about IQ and more interested in actualizing potential.)

Researchers have maintained for years that human beings use but a small amount of their overall intelligence or brain capacity. The figure usually seems to hover somewhere around ten percent. Since intelligence is associated with awareness and comprehension, imagine what life would be like if we used the other 90% of our capacity! I'm reminded of Shakespeare's tragic play *Hamlet,* in which the Prince of Denmark declares, "Lord, we know what we are, but know not what we may be."

Point of View

In the inner world we can open to the *sky of mind,* where there is no limit to awareness. At the higher altitudes of our inner atmosphere, we find air that is pure and rarefied. Ideas and thoughts that come from these altitudes are pristine and clear. At the lower altitudes, however, we often find mental smog and clouds of dark, turbulent thought.

The voices we hear inside our mind have various points of view, reflecting the differences of inner altitude. The playwright, director, and actors all perceive life from different levels of consciousness. These views range all the way from the clear knowing of the playwright to the absolute ignorance of some actors. (Note the various levels in the sidebar on this page.)

When you speak, who inside holds this view? Listen to *who's* talking. Is it the soul's perspective, the director's, or that of an actor? And when you speak, ask yourself: "What's the real truth?" Is what you are saying a truth that is universally recognized, a personal conviction, or a half-truth? Does what you say ring true?

The first step of directing requires a willingness to recognize your unconscious patterns of behavior and to see what *is* rather than what

PLAYWRIGHT'S AWARENESS
Universal Truth
fully awake
illuminated, enlightened
infinite mind
infinite creativity
infinite silence

△

DIRECTOR'S AWARENESS
personal truth
personal awareness
intuitive knowing
objective observer
visionary
wise

△

ACTOR'S AWARENESS
(ACCOMPLISHED)
rational
common sense
discerning
honest
perceptive
humorous
realistic
open minded
understanding

△

(UNACCOMPLISHED)
irrational
ignorant/confused
critical/cynical
deceptive/lying
judgmental
sarcastic
self-righteous
prejudiced
misunderstanding

*Have an open mind, but
not so open that
your brains fall out.*
JACOB NEEDLEMAN

you want something to be. Asking that the real truth be revealed in your daily life takes courage, but if you are willing to do so, the result is expansive and freeing. The dreary alternative is to find yourself in a room full of mirrors, seeing nothing more than what you want to see, feeling nothing more than what you already feel. The mirror, mirror on the wall reflects the guises of us all.

The Good, the Bad, and the Ugly

As you observe your players, you'll notice that some conduct themselves in ways that are useful and some do not. Some block your progress, drain your energy, create confusion, or dispute your love. A few may even try to destroy the play you are producing. Fortunately, you also have valiant actors who forge through the thickets of self-defense to pursue creativity, see humor in the absurd, risk relationships, and take responsibility.

Each actor expresses a particular quality *and* a particular need of your personality. Each tries to meet its own needs the best way it knows. When the needs of actors are met, they play their parts effortlessly. They feel that life is as it should be. These *accomplished* players are creative and alive, because they have scripts that are juicy, vital, and rewarding.

When the needs of certain actors are *not* met, they are forced to adapt to the situations at hand. They do the best they can, but not knowing how to act, they imitate the actions of others or pretend to be someone they are not. Hiding real feelings of fear, anger, sadness, or even love and affection, they try to fit into other people's expectations. The results are performances that mark these players as struggling and *unaccomplished*.

Unaccomplished actors are those who are either undeveloped or maladjusted. They have not *yet* learned to play their parts well. *Undeveloped* characters could include the beginning Tennis Player, the first-time Traveler, or the budding Artist. Nothing is "wrong" with these players; they are just learning new skills. *Maladjusted* actors, by contrast, could include the Dictator, Manipulator, Couch Potato, Cynic, or Clinging Vine. They express an unbalanced stance toward life. They may play their parts very well, but their mind, heart, and will are not integrated. For example, the Dictator and Manipulator may have brains and power, but lack heart. The Couch Potato is very good-natured and relaxed, but lacks will. The Clinging Vine has a heartfelt attachment to a relationship, but lacks inner strength and wisdom.

When you listen to your inner voices, attend to *what* wants to be said and *who* wants to say it. Listen to the tone and volume of each voice as it changes with every actor. For example, when you congratu-

Those who follow the part of themselves that is great will become great; those who follow the part of themselves that is small will become small.
MENCIUS

Cynicism is humor in ill-health.
H. G. WELLS

*If you judge people, you
have no time to love them.*
MOTHER TERESA

late yourself for something you did well, notice which part is congratu-lating and which part is being congratulated. When you feel like kicking yourself for having done something you regard as foolish, notice which part is kicking and which is being kicked. Put both parts on the stage in front of you and observe their behavior—*without judging*!

This discussion raised questions for one friend who said: "I'm perfectly aware that I have an inner Sadist. Now, should I regard him as a basically bad character who ought not be let onto the stage at all? Or should I regard him as a perversion of, say, my Passionate Creator, who, when blocked, oozes unpleasantly through the seams? Or should I seek to *dissolve* my Sadist through insight and understanding, recognizing that he is in me, even while I work to diminish his presence and power until he disappears? Do I seek to *balance* him, seeking to make him a healthy Sadist, not given to hurting people but willing to squash a few bugs now and then to relieve tension?"

In answering questions like this one, I usually suggest that the first step is simply to *recognize* who is present—in this case, a Sadist who is living inside. Then you'll want to become better acquainted with him, to discover more details: How does he act? What does he wear? How big is he? When does he come out? What does he say? These questions will help you identify the actor more precisely.

Many of these issues will be addressed when we discuss the second and third steps of directing. We're taking one step at a time right now, so you'll know exactly what the director needs to do in the beginning. (But, here's a little clue regarding the end goal for an inner Sadist: the director's goal will not be to help the Sadist become a star Sadist. Rather, it will be to help him discover his *real* purpose in the production. He does have one! And it's a positive contribution! It's up to you as the director to discover what it is.)

How do you know if you're playing the part of an accomplished or unaccomplished actor?

You know you are playing the part of an unaccomplished or amateur actor when you . . .

   . . . are fearful;

   . . . are confused or "in the dark";

   . . . are unwilling to look at yourself or your relationships;

   . . . are unable to see beyond your own needs;

   . . . don't change even when your way is ineffective;

   . . . manipulate others to get your way;

   . . . misrepresent the truth;

   . . . dominate or control others and situations;

   . . . over-act or try to make an impression;

   . . . get your "buttons" pushed;

   . . . feel stuck, imprisoned, or degraded;

   . . . feel separate, abandoned, or like you don't belong;

   . . . feel powerless, depressed, or victimized;

   . . . feel driven or addicted;

   . . . have no purpose or meaning.

You can tell that you are playing the part of an *accomplished* actor when you . . .

   . . . are loving;

   . . . are honest and open to the truth;

   . . . express your emotions freely;

   . . . accept yourself and others;

   . . . take full responsibility for your actions;

   . . . experience freedom and inner power;

   . . . use your talents creatively;

   . . . are willing to make mistakes and take risks;

   . . . express intelligence, love, and will.

There is no better way to encourage excellence in people than to treat them as if they are already great.
G. RADBRUCH

The Star

Something magical happens when a star actor is in the spotlight. Attention from the audience evokes something strong and excellent from within. There is a hush. A palpable expectancy. An enchanting communion. The actor's strong aura envelops the audience, which sits spellbound. Breathless. Ah, the Star! Luminous presence. Embodied excellence.

We watch as Olympic athletes win gold medals. We want the ice skaters to do well. We want the skiers to be flawless. In the cinema, we watch as a movie actor plays a scene exquisitely, with feeling and sensitivity. We want her to do her best. *We want people to excel!*

Why should it be any different in your inner theatre? Why not give your own inner stars special accolades and attention? Why not coach and support their blossoming talents?

But who are your stars? Who in your cast deserves bouquets of flowers?

When I ask those questions, people often squirm. We're not used to thinking of ourselves in that way. We're more used to putting ourselves down for not being good enough. Rarely do we give ourselves applause for being really good.

Actually, accomplished actors are the parts of us that seem so natural, we tend to think of them as "no big deal." Among people who have attended my workshops, the following are some of the star actors that have come forward: the competent Organizer who knows how to get things done; the Sister of Mercy who feels deep compassion for people; the Strong-Woman-Drumming who evokes the fire-energy from down deep and brings her fresh vitality and power. Others include the attentive Gardener, the skilled Builder, and the graceful Dancer who flows like water.

Perhaps your accomplished actor is a creative Computer Programmer, a brilliant Diplomat, a great Storyteller, or a colorful Clothing Designer. Whatever your star's talent, you feel good about yourself because of that ability. You feel gratification and satisfaction.

In considering your talents, you may (as many people do) feel embarrassed about admitting that you are really good in some area. At times you may even put on dark glasses to keep others from seeing your true genius. Some people may keep a star actor secluded backstage so they can fit in more easily with the mediocrity of those around them.

This is a sad waste of talent, since stars sleeping backstage hold the strength and motivation you might otherwise have available for great accomplishments. They hold your deep love, purity, and innocence. They hold your knowledge and expertise. They hold your beauty and spirituality. And there they are—asleep! Author Marianne Williamson says, "Your playing small does not serve the world. There is nothing enlightened about shrinking so that other people won't feel insecure around you." So shrinking is not the answer! Instead, we must shine our brightest. Williamson explains that "as we let our own Light shine, we unconsciously give other people permission to do the same."

When you ignore your stars, you project their qualities onto other people. You recognize *their* greatness but deny it in yourself. Think about this: who inside you recognizes these qualities? Is it not true that if you didn't have the same capacities within yourself, you wouldn't be able to perceive them in others? There's more truth than most of us realize in the old saying, "It takes one to know one."

Star qualities can also be called *spiritual* qualities, since they connect you with what is most essentially yourself. At the core of all your actors, if you look deep enough, you'll find a gleaming quality of soul. Your recognition of that quality will call it forth.

When I think of evoking qualities, I think of a poignant segment of the film *Don Juan DeMarco*. Don Juan, who believes he is the world's greatest lover, is committed to a mental hospital because of his apparent delusions of grandeur. Dressed in a gallant Spanish costume, Don Juan shares his beliefs about women with his psychiatrist. He reflects: "It is a matter of perception. Some may say that one woman may have a nose that is too large, or another feature that is too small, but I do not look at those things at all. I see the radiant jewel that lives within each woman, the gorgeous, unique beauty at her core, and she responds to my vision by expressing that great beauty, because that is what I see."

Hearing this, I also fell in love with Don Juan. He seemed to see the deeper truth in women, regardless of their appearance. No wonder he had such a powerful effect on the female population!

In the republic of mediocrity, genius is dangerous.
ROBERT INGERSOLL

Wasted talents are crimes against the soul.
UTA HAGEN

STAR QUALITIES
Appreciation
Acceptance
Beauty
Calm
Compassion
Confidence
Contentment
Cooperation
Courage
Creativity
Devotion
Enthusiasm
Energy
Faith
Freedom
Friendship
Generosity
Grace
Gratitude
Harmony
Honor
Honesty
Humor
Innocence
Inspiration
Joy
Kindness
Light
Love
Loyalty
Order
Patience
Power
Peace
Purity
Service
Simplicity
Stillness
Strength
Trust
Truth
Understanding

When you see the "radiant jewel" that lives within each actor, the "unique beauty" at their core, they, too, will respond by expressing their star qualities. They will shine, and because they shine, they will be called *stars*.

Gabrielle Roth, in her book *Maps to Ecstasy,* explains that our "authentic roles in life are not the bit parts of the ego's melodramas, but the archetypes of the soul." She goes on to say that the "soul enacts these qualities in creative interplay with oneself, others, and the world. And it opens the way for a life grounded in the spirit."

Celebrating the qualities of your top stars and giving them the honor they deserve is important. When you do so, you encourage all your actors to develop their talents and express their gifts. You can even ask your most expert players to instruct the struggling ones. The strong can support the weak.

Recognizing a Star Actor

Sit down in your director's chair and stay alert as you objectively observe the part of your life that is going well. What do you do easily and successfully? Put this part of yourself on stage. Notice how natural and effortless your activity appears to be when you play this role.

✎ *In a notebook or journal, use the following outline to create a dialogue between you and your star actor. Listen as your actor gives you information about who it is.*

DIRECTOR: What part of life is going well? What do you do easily?
ACTOR: The thing I do well is . . .
DIRECTOR: What role do you play in our production?
ACTOR: I'm playing the role of . . .
DIRECTOR: How do you look? (Costume, age, gender, size, shape)
ACTOR:
DIRECTOR: How do you act? (Habits, gestures, stance, movement)
ACTOR:
DIRECTOR: What do you feel? (Moods, emotions)
ACTOR: Most of the time I feel . . .
DIRECTOR: What do you think about? (Thoughts, fantasies, beliefs)
ACTOR:

DIRECTOR: What do you say? (Usual statements, tone of voice)
ACTOR:
DIRECTOR: What star quality do you contribute to our show?
ACTOR:
DIRECTOR: What background music might accompany your act?
ACTOR:
DIRECTOR: What's your name?
ACTOR:
DIRECTOR: What's the name of this play?
ACTOR: The name of this play is . . .

Sketch a picture of this star actor.

Use what talents you possess; the woods would be very silent if no birds sang there except those that sang best.
HENRY VAN DYKE

Lela's Star Actor

Brushing long, blonde hair behind her ear with weathered fingers, Lela tells a workshop group about her star in the spotlight. Lela's star plays the role of a house designer and builder. Looking a lot like Lela, the star is around 46 years old, about 5'9", has a strong build, uses muted makeup, and dresses with great creativity.

Her name is "Indy," for Independent Woman. She is very business-like, and her actions express self-assurance, flexibility, caring, and excitement. She feels at ease, confident, pretty, casual, happy, and intense.

Indy believes that if she asks the universe for something, she will receive it. She says things like: "Ask for what you want" and "Commit to pursuing what you love."

What does she contribute to the world? She designs and builds beautiful, artistic homes for people. As a good partner, she includes others in her projects.

The music that accompanies her production is Celtic, South African, Hawaiian, or Irish.

The name of her play is *Beautiful Lifestyle.*

The Amateur Actor

Amateur or unaccomplished actors are the parts of ourselves we don't
like very much. These actors are doing the best they can, but they
haven't *yet* developed their star qualities.

For many actors, the special talent or gift they are born to express
remains hidden behind masks and layers of costumes. Many such actors
are unaware that they have a special star quality waiting to be developed. Some believe they are wicked at the core, while others think they
are basically no good. These actors confuse themselves with their fear
and their bumbling actions.

Untrained players, not *yet* knowing their script, stumble over their
lines. Not *yet* knowing when to make their entrances and exits, they
impulsively barge onto the stage and disrupt performances. Many enact
parts that belong to others, and almost all unconsciously act out roles
that have been passed down through generations. Some of the most
unfortunate have been twisted by their suffering and pain.

Who are these unaccomplished actors? Adam's actor is the
Trembling Tree who is afraid of establishing intimate relationships with
other people. Paovo's is the Skeleton who believes it's "too late" to
live. Kasha's is the rejected Child who cries in the rain. And Thomas
has to deal with his angry Enragé who wears a black mask with a red,
jagged streak and lashes out at others.

Perhaps you have an unaccomplished actor who's afraid to talk to
people, or one who believes it's too old, ugly, fat, skinny, short, or tall.
You may have one who is depressed, perpetually intoxicated, deceptive, or abusive.

When actors' needs are not met, they compete and fight with each
other. The General humiliates the Soldier, the Fanatic hates the
Unbeliever, the Playboy frustrates the Monk, the Wild Woman scares
the Housewife. If these actors aren't given new scripts, they'll continue
their old, unhappy song and dance.

And why is all of this a problem? One big reason: when you
identify with a struggling actor, you think *you* are your pain; you
believe *you* are the problem. You feel discouraged. You're definitely
not having fun *yet*.

Listen to how Ram Dass explained it. "As long as you are in a role—any role at all: sexy, young, male, female, married, single, needful, ex-alcoholic or in recovery, whatever definition you have—it is a trap if you are caught in it." When you're trapped in a role, you feel as though you have no choice to change and consequently, you create a *big* drama around yourself. However, if you realize that you are simply playing a role, then you can play that role as a free and conscious participant. Or as Ram Dass said, "It is not a trap if you are merely celebrating the Universe through participating in it."

This is the difference between a drama and a play.

It is a well-recognized fact that *a problem cannot be resolved at the same level on which it was created.* Actors can't change by themselves: the Miser can't attract wealth; the Worrier can't control the stock market; the Dominator can't elicit cooperation; and the Addict can't say "no" to drugs. These actors are unable to change by themselves because they need the director's larger perspective and greater power to help them out of their old gig.

But take heart! This is the natural process of growth. In theatre rehearsals, as in life, none of the cast knows what to say or how to act when they're first given a script. All have to practice their parts and learn effective methods of acting. Your struggling actors need help to become the stars they are meant to be. They need to rehearse and develop their potential talents. They don't have to learn by themselves.

They say you should not suffer through the past. You should be able to wear it like a loose garment, take it off and let it drop.
EVA JESSYE

Recognizing an Unaccomplished Actor

Return to your director's chair and observe the area of your life in which you experience the greatest amount of suffering. Step back from the part that's struggling and put that actor on stage.

✍ *Create a script allowing the actor to give you information about itself and its problem. Use the following format to guide your dialogue.*

DIRECTOR: What part of life is not fun? What is the problem?
ACTOR: My problem is . . .
DIRECTOR: What role are you playing?
ACTOR: I'm playing the role of . . .
DIRECTOR: How do you look? (costume, age, gender, size, shape)
ACTOR:

DIRECTOR: How do you act? (Habits, gestures, stance, movement)
ACTOR:
DIRECTOR: What do you feel? (Moods, emotions)
ACTOR:
DIRECTOR: What do you think about? (Thoughts, fantasies, beliefs)
ACTOR:
DIRECTOR: What do you say? (Usual statements, tone of voice)
ACTOR:
DIRECTOR: What happened to cause your suffering? (Script, story)
ACTOR:
DIRECTOR: What music accompanies your act?
ACTOR:
DIRECTOR: What's your name?
ACTOR:
DIRECTOR: What's the name of this play?
ACTOR:

Sketch a picture of your unaccomplished actor.

*Our secret selves lie
hidden beneath the
deceptive smoothness
of our skin. . . And if we
dare plunge deeply into
the hidden recesses of
our souls, we find
old gods and witches,
children, torturers
and friends.*
DEANNA SCLAR

Anna's First Step in Directing

Anna, a school teacher in Germany, serves as an example of how one person took an actor through all three steps of directing. Here she made the first step by *recognizing* an actor.

Anna came to me complaining that she had had too much work to do—too many appointments, too many pressures from others. When I asked her to step back from the suffering part and put it on stage in front of the two of us, she had no trouble doing so. She pulled up a chair for her directing-self and another one for her tired actor. As she moved from one chair to the other, the following dialogue unfolded:

DIRECTOR: What's the problem?
ACTOR: My problem is the feeling of not doing enough, of not having enough time.
DIRECTOR: What role are you playing?
ACTOR: I'm playing the role of someone who is stressed out.

DIRECTOR: How do you look? What do you wear?

ACTOR: I'm about 35 years old, male, about 6 feet tall, and a bit overweight. My shoulders are rounded. I wear a dark suit that isn't ironed. A button is lost and there are stains. I wear expensive patent leather shoes, which aren't clean.

DIRECTOR: How do you act?

ACTOR: I am nervous and I often run around searching for something I left somewhere. I often look at the clock. I shake my head and shrug my shoulders. I make fists, rub my chin, or cover my face with my hands. I frown. I walk fast and my steps can be heard. I gobble down my food.

DIRECTOR: What do you feel?

ACTOR: I feel tense and I'm often depressed. I feel heavy. I live in a gray zone. I have no time for laughter.

DIRECTOR: What do you think?

ACTOR: I think life is just effort. When something goes easy, it isn't worthwhile or valuable. I think I need to be a hard-working person. With hard work, much more would be possible. I could be more successful if I worked harder. I believe the day doesn't have enough hours. I have to work hard to make money and have a career and be socially recognized. Taking breaks and relaxing is a waste of time. If people worked harder, we could solve problems on our planet.

DIRECTOR: What do you say?

ACTOR: "If I had more time, I could accomplish much more." And, "I can find a solution if I work hard enough on it." My voice is high, shrill, and often loud. I speak too fast and in feeble tones.

DIRECTOR: Describe the incident or incidents that caused your suffering.

ACTOR: In my childhood, my parents ran a restaurant. They were very busy and showed me that the only way to have a secure life, with enough money, was to work very hard. To be a valuable member of the family and community, you had to work hard. Leisure time was very rare. Playing was a luxury. When I was ten, I was the size of an adult. It became clear to me that to get recognition, I needed to do something useful. I never had enough time to sleep or play.

DIRECTOR: What music accompanies your act?

ACTOR: A brass band plays military marches.
DIRECTOR: What is your name?
ACTOR: My name is *Stressman*.

Anna has now taken the first step of directing by identifying her struggling actor. Later, she will come back and take Stressman through the next steps.

Demons and Dragons

While we're partially aware of some of our undesirable characters, others are completely alien to our conscious image of ourselves. We don't like to admit it, but within each of us there are shady characters living in underground labyrinths. Behind the scenes and out of sight, these actors drive us to impulsive action . . . or they may sabotage our whole show.

All of us, in spite of our ethics and high morals, are capable of terrible actions if we are pushed far enough. War pushes people to that limit, conjuring up the most vicious demons of all. In the film, *The Killing Fields,* we see young boys who would normally be playing games together become little savages as they taunt their captives then blow their brains out.

Even *before* we are pushed to the breaking point, we experience our villains running around inside. They tell little white lies, cheat on income taxes, break the speed limit, and manipulate others to get their own way. Fear, greed, hatred, revenge, and selfishness are emotions we all know and have learned to mask.

Even good, religious people have a dark side. A minister's wife tells of the night she was lying in bed beside her sleeping husband. The thought came to her to stab him in the heart with an ice pick. Mortified that she even had such a thought ("Since I'm really a very good woman"), she asked herself *why* this idea had popped into her mind. Ice pick . . . stabbing . . . heart . . . what did it mean? Then she knew. She felt that her husband's heart was as cold as ice. What she really wanted was to chip away the ice and get to the love that was frozen inside.

Someone less aware might have acted on the murderous impulse instead of discovering the deeper meaning of the emotion. Fortunately for the minister, his wife was not really a Killer-Bitch and was able to acknowledge her feelings of desperation in the relationship.

Who are the inner villains? They are the dark characters made up of all the negative thoughts and feelings that you deny and pretend don't exist. They may show up in your dreams as the Phantom (like the *Phantom of the Opera*), a giant Bull, a Monster, a fire-breathing Dragon, or a cloaked figure lurking in the shadows. They may appear as a "wolf in sheep's clothing" or as a white-robed, self-righteous god.

It does not do to leave a live dragon out of your calculations if you live near him.
J. R. R. TOLKIEN

Every man's enemy is within himself.
BAHYA

Regardless of how twisted or threatening these actors may seem, they are *not* your enemy. They play important roles in your production, for they are, after all, parts of you and they need to be seen with clarity and discernment. They can be dangerous, but they all have a purpose.

The purpose of your dark actors (also referred to in psychology as the "shadow") is to collect all the experiences you don't know how to handle and to hold their *charged feelings* until you are able to resolve them. You may catch glimpses of your shadow-actors reflected in the eyes of someone whom you judge, blame, or hate, since recognizing the Beast or the Enemy in someone else is often easier than to see it in yourself. Your so-called enemies in the outer world may be *reflections* of what is imprisoned in your own dungeon. When strong, negative feelings pop up without warning, those emotions may indicate that something inside *you* is not resolved.

My friend Madelaine remembered how her father used to tell her stories about terrible witches when she was small. Terrorized by his dramatic enactment of their cackling and their sinister aspects, she tried hard not to think about them. Then one day Madelaine decided to take a hike into the deep forest of her subconscious. Her intention was to search for parts of herself she had disowned. Deep in the forest, she came upon a cabin, and who should appear but a cloaked, ugly, wart-nosed Witch. Frightened, Madelaine had the impulse to turn and run, but then she remembered—even though she didn't yet understand who the Witch was—that the cloaked one was a lost part of herself. Regaining her composure, Madelaine stood firm and faced the Witch. To her surprise, this led to her uncovering a startling truth.

MADELAINE: Witch, it's time for you and me to face off.

WITCH: Don't underestimate me. I am more powerful than you imagine.

MADELAINE: I believe you are, and I believe I am more powerful than *you* imagine. God's light is shining through me even in your dark cottage. I want to be partners with you and to eventually be loving friends. I believe you have much wisdom to share with me.

WITCH: I have much wisdom indeed. Are you worthy?

MADELAINE: Yes.

WITCH: Okay. Your first lesson is this: *In the darkness, there is light.*

MADELAINE: Tell me more.

WITCH: Before I tell you more, you must take time to contemplate and perceive my messages clearly.

That was her first encounter with her inner Witch. Eventually Madelaine brought her out of the forest and gave her a dressing room in her inner theatre. She realized that years ago she had disowned her intuitive, feminine wisdom (a quality of men as well as women), and that her angry, denied part had taken on the classic characteristics of a Witch. In other words, when her inner Wise Woman was denied, a part of her went underground and turned into an ugly, bitchy Witch.

Surprised by this insight, Madelaine said to me: "When I met the Witch and found that she really loved me and wanted to help, I asked her to sit on my right side and lend me her wisdom. Among other things, she has expertise in street smarts and knows how to assess danger."

In the beginning, Madelaine wondered if the Witch was an archetype, and if so, would she be able to change her? I shared my belief that *true archetypes* are the perfected patterns for what inner characters can become, while *actors* are imperfections of the archetypes. Actors are in training to fulfill their archetypal patterns. They have lots of room for growth. And, while you can't improve an archetype (an already perfect pattern), you can improve an actor (an imperfect pattern of behavior). So, when Madelaine's Wise Old Woman (a true archetype) was betrayed—when she disowned her intuitive, feminine wisdom—a part of Madelaine became witchy and scary and angry. In other words, her ugly Witch-actor was born.

Disowned actors are not happy campers. They do not take lightly to being ignored. When I think of people's suppressed actors, I think of Mack, a pragmatic credit manager living in southern California. Mack considered going back to school to study psychology. This was so different from the type of work he was involved in that his whole cast went into a tizzy. Indeed, a group of his actors were interested and eager to change vocational direction, but there was also a group he called *the bad-ass ringleaders* who seemed to have a different opinion. I asked him to call them onto the stage to see who they were. They appeared and, in Mac's colorful and explicit words, they included:

The lower side of me so recently chained down, began to growl for license.
DR. JEKYLL
(ROBERT L. STEVENSON)

Clyde, the bastard, who is a Hell's Angel. He always carries a beer in one hand and a cigarette in the other. He wears a T-shirt and jeans with the crack in his ass showing. He has bushy hair and is balding on top.

Izzy, a depraved, skinny fart. He has splotchy zits and wears a pink-and-white shirt. He's a sneaky slimeball. He stays more sober than the others so he can steal. He's also paranoid.

Ralph, a.k.a. *Fat Albert*, who wears jeans and suspenders. He's a glutton—a bottomless pit. He doesn't smoke or play around with women.

Evelyn, or "*Elly*," the town whore. She rats her hair and doesn't wash it very often. She wears a white mini-dress and white bobby socks. She has a good build but a bad face. She smokes, drinks, and raises hell. She smells bad.

Floyd is a phony son of a bitch who nails everything in town. He's superficial, slick, and avoids confrontations. He's scared of relationships and is narcissistic.

When these actors appeared, Mack was ready to fire them all, but I asked him to hold off, to step into his director's chair, and to listen to what they had to say. I knew that if Mack continued to deny his "bad-ass" players, he'd give up his power to change. If he acknowledged them, he would be able to take charge of their behavior. (You will hear more about Mack later.)

There's no way around it. At some point, we have to take responsibility for our demons and dragons. When we feel intolerant, we have the opportunity to admit we have an inner Bigot. When we feel crude, we have to admit that a Beavis or Butt-head lives inside of us. *Huh, huh, huh.* (I still cringe when I think of them living inside of me!) And, of course, when we feel like murdering someone, we need to recognize our inner Torturer or Killer.

Viktor Frankl, whom we met in an earlier chapter, observed that "once the angel in us is repressed, he turns into a demon." Knowing that our inner demons are fallen angels can make paying attention to them easier. If we perceive them as being *afraid, twisted,* or *incomplete,* we can feel compassion instead of being judgmental.

We don't have to suffer to change, but if we don't change we will suffer. We can't wait for our disliked parts to just go away. The only way to change a villain is to stop running, look it in the eyes, then take it in our arms and love it once again. Yes, even the monsters and dragons. They, too, will sit in our lap—*if* we expand our consciousness to include them.

Our devilish characters hold part of the dreams and visions for our play. They are disowned parts waiting to be recognized. They want to be a part of the show! Actually, *they are in training to become gods and goddesses themselves*. Even Terrorists and Killers can be redeemed or transformed. They, too, can become gods someday. That's because badness is not an end state. To reiterate: the task of the director is to help actors change bad acting so they can express their potential star qualities.

As Polish theatre director Jerzy Grotowski pointed out, "Just as a great sinner can become a saint . . . the actor's wretchedness can be transformed into a kind of holiness." In other words, our worst villains can become "holy actors."

Those who have not met their inner demons will not be able to take part in building a more open society.
PIERO FERRUCCI

Second Step in Directing

AS DIRECTOR, I ESTABLISH A RELATIONSHIP WITH MY ACTORS
AND ACCEPT THEIR INNERMOST NEEDS.

SECOND STEP INVOLVES
Acceptance
Resonance
Cohesion
Emotions
Empathy
Affection
Feelings
Caring
Heart
Love

There is only one kind of love, but there are a thousand different versions.
LAROCHEFOUCAULD

The most profound relationship we'll ever have is the one with ourselves.
SHIRLEY MACLAINE

By recognizing some of your inner actors, you've now taken the first step in directing your play. In observing their patterns of behavior, you've already begun to change your performance. According to quantum physics, an observer influences that which is observed; the witness is actually a participant. As the producer-director, your very awareness changes things!

However, there's more to directing than simply witnessing who and what is on the stage. The second step in directing involves opening your heart and *accepting your actors;* in other words, it's about loving your selves. Love is a wonderful and mysterious happening, and you'll discover that you have as many different kinds of love as you have members of your entourage.

The playwright, director, and actors all have different capacities for love. The playwright's Love is *unconditional* (given regardless of circumstances) and *inclusive* (encompassing all parts of the personality). It is *cohesive* (holding the show together), *unifying* (bringing the actors into relationship), and *resonant* (establishing natural order and harmony).

The director becomes a conduit for this incredible love, which is registered by the mind, intensified by the emotions, and expressed through the body. As the directing-self, one *personalizes* love by having a loving attitude, by feeling loving emotions, and by acting in loving ways.

Our actors are a bit different. They are here to feel all the variations of human emotion. In the same way that each actor has a mind of its own, each also has a heart of its own. At best, the love of the inner Parent, for example, is nurturing and protective; the Child's love is innocent and trusting; the Lover's is romantic and erotic; the Manager's is concerned and caring; and the Mystic's is pure and spiritual.

To produce a successful play, you will want to feel and own the depth of *all* your feelings. You may be surprised to discover that "if you are able to go deep, you will find that every emotion turns out to be love in disguise," as Deepak Chopra observes.

For the Love of Actors

The moment you become aware of an actor, you automatically establish a relationship with this part of yourself. As with every relationship, you immediately register an emotional response: relief, anger, revulsion, compassion, delight, fear, embarrassment, empathy, or any of dozens more. Each actor evokes something different in you when it appears in the spotlight.

The quality of relationship you establish with an actor depends on your ability to extend love. Our human show depends on love for its existence. It depends on the magnetic attraction of the heart to heal wounded actors, reconcile broken relationships, and unify the cast. Love is the glue that holds your personality together.

As director, you have the task of making a heartfelt connection with your actors, for without love, the show has no cohesion or integrity. Without heart, the show is cold, passionless, and even brutal. If your heart is not in your performance, the show has no real meaning.

Oprah Winfrey once said to her television audience, "You're either moving in the direction of love or in the direction of fear." She's right! Love and fear are the two basic emotions we experience. We can choose to open our hearts to our actors and other people or to close down in fear. We can embrace or we can reject. Both are viable options, but the drama of simply protecting ourselves can become very boring. At some point, we realize that taking the risk of loving is much more interesting. Love makes life worth living.

You need not be afraid of loving yourself too much. No one ever died from an overdose of love. "But," you may ask, "what about narcissism?" True enough, your inner Narcissus may have a love affair with his own image, but he is an actor who needs your love the same as all the others. When you give him the love he seeks, his endless fascination with his image will come to an end. Let go of your worry that loving your selves will somehow cause you to be excessively self-involved or uninterested in relating to others. What you'll discover is that the more you love your inner selves, the more you'll be able to love the other human beings in your life.

PLAYWRIGHT'S LOVE
unconditional
inclusive
nourishing
cohesive
unifying
resonant
abundant
♡

DIRECTOR'S LOVE
personal
harmonizing
impartial
accepting
compassionate
empathetic
grateful
♡

ACTOR'S LOVE
(ACCOMPLISHED)
conditional
caring
passionate
generous
affectionate
tender
considerate
patient
appreciative
gracious
♡

(UNACCOMPLISHED)
selfish
withholding
indifferent
possessive
sentimental
jealous
seductive
impatient
rejecting
hateful
fearful

Love as Resonance

Love holds the secret to success and happiness. Poets, mystics, and philosophers have understood this for ages, and now some scientists are attempting to understand the energy of love.

Energetically, every member of your entourage has a specific vibration differentiating him or her from all the others. Just as every color and sound has its own frequency, every distinct part of us (cell, organ, emotion, actor) has its own vibratory signature. Essentially, each member contributes a particular hue and tone to the production.

When people relate to one another, they send and receive messages through the waves of their vibrations. If two or more people are on the same wavelength (if one frequency matches the other), they come into *resonance*. In other words, if the people understand each other or share the same feelings, they—as one popular phrasing has it—get each other's "vibes."

This is something you experience every day. You feel resonance when someone "sees" you, when someone "feels" your feeling, or when someone "gets" who you are. In his book *Healing with Love*, Dr. Leonard Laskow explains that *love is the resonance in a relationship*. Resonance is what occurs when you fall in love and feel as though you and your lover are the only two people in the world, or when you are holding your child and the bond between you is so strong that it brings tears to your eyes, or when you sign a business contract and your partner lets you know that he realizes how much the deal means to you by giving you a firm handshake.

Love is a high-frequency energy. It's so powerful that it can influence the most stubborn person, or melt the heart of the most hardened employee. This occurs because higher frequencies penetrate lower frequencies. When you send forth a loving thought (a very high frequency), the person receives it instantly, regardless of distance or how many walls are between you. Since there are no barriers to love, it is absorbed even if the other person is unaware of having received it. Love penetrates. Love strengthens. Love heals.

Qualities such as love, gratitude, joy, and acceptance have higher vibrations than those of fear, malice, greed, and hate. When you're feeling depressed or "down," you feel heavy, slow, and dark. If you begin to think of all the things for which you are grateful, or if you think of all the people you love, you soon notice a change in your energy level. You feel lighter and more energized. You just feel better. Negativity is neutralized when love is present. More than that, it is transformed.

Like an acorn that holds the growth pattern of the oak, the heart of each actor holds the potential for what it may be. This potential star-quality has a specific frequency, or natural vibration. If actors are true to themselves, they naturally develop and express their unique qualities. If they get off-track or out of sync, they have a difficult time finding their own style and voice. Something is unnatural. As director, you have the responsibility to *come into resonance* with the actor's essence and evoke its natural expression.

How do you do this?

To come into resonance with the actor, you must open your heart, create a safe space on the stage, and embrace this part of yourself. Your heart knows how. You can trust it. Your heart sends out "feeler waves" to discover the thoughts and feelings of this actor as precisely as possible. To come into resonance, you try to "feel for" or "get the vibes" of the other. In other words, you want to have *empathy*.

How can you tell when you're on the same wavelength?

You know you're on the same frequency when the actor says: "Ah ha! That's exactly how I feel," or "Yes, that's it. I get the connection!" This is what it means to understand your self. It's *you* understanding one of your *selves*. It's *you* standing by your *self*.

When this happens, the two of you are "in phase" or "in step." When you are in step with each other, only a minimum amount of energy is required to produce maximum change. In other words, your actor *wants to change* because there's no longer any reason to resist, to doubt, or to rebel.

Actors' Needs

Actors have human needs they try to fulfill. To come into resonance with an actor, you'll want to clarify what it needs in its heart-of-hearts. Some actors may be concerned about their basic needs, while others may be seeking transcendent fulfillment. Psychologist Abraham

Go to your bosom, knock there and ask your heart what it doth know.
SHAKESPEARE

It is not your intellect which will bring you home, it is your heart which will bring you home.
PTAAH

Maslow developed a "hierarchy of needs" that can help you determine what your actors want. The following is adapted from Maslow's hierarchy.

Without the transcendent and the transpersonal, we get sick, violent and nihilistic, or else hopeless and apathetic.
MASLOW

Self-transcendence
Need to contribute to humanity.
Need to transcend personal concerns.
Need to commit to something greater than self.
Need to see one's place in the larger Play.

Self-actualization
Need to develop and fulfill one's potential.
Need to enjoy work and be productive.
Need to be self-directing.
Need for truth, beauty, and justice.

Self-esteem
Need to be respected by self and others.
Need to feel confident and capable.
Need to feel worthy.
Need to have power and influence.

Love and belonging
Need for affection and touching.
Need to express oneself freely.
Need to belong and to be loved by family and group.
Need for intimacy with a partner.

Safety and security
Need to feel secure and protected.
Need to be free from danger.
Need for predictable future.
Need to have stability and order.

. . . man's higher nature is inconceivable without a satisfied lower nature as a base.
MASLOW

Basic physiological needs
Need for food, water, shelter.
Need for sleep, relaxation.
Need for sex, exercise.
Need for relief from pain.

A New Way of Loving

Loving your selves means accepting the *best* and *worst* of your personality. It means being open to everything in your experience, both good and bad, without blame or rejection. This means being vulnerable and providing a safe place for all the players to come forth.

But *what,* exactly, are you accepting? *What* are you allowing? Do you accept your actors' uncivilized behaviors? Do you unlock the prison doors and allow your captives to wreak havoc on the stage? Do you let the pity-part play its violin solo? Do you permit your wounded Warrior to bloody the platform?

As director, you don't accept an actor's poor performance, nor do you allow a character to run wild. Permitting your cast to wallow in negative feelings or to give a poor performance is *not* a loving thing to do. What *is* loving is to see deep into the actor's heart, where you will find its core need. This central need is really the actor's *potential* star quality, which is waiting to be developed and expressed.

The needs themselves are not really a problem. The problem is the *way* actors unwittingly try to satisfy their needs. Players try to get what they want by whining, resisting, dominating, pretending, and manipulating. They *act out,* because they have not *yet* learned a better way to satisfy their heart's deepest desires.

For example, you'll discover that the Rebel's deepest need is *independence*, but not knowing how to achieve this, he becomes defiant, insubordinate, and resistant. Think of the actors in a medieval kingdom. You'll discover that the stern, autocratic King really, in his heart, wants true *power.* The possessive, jealous Queen really wants *love.* The vain, self-absorbed Princess simply wants deep *recognition.* The zealous, fanatic Knight wants an *ideal mission.* The driven, mad Alchemist wants to experience the "Ah-ha" of *discovery.* And the ridiculous, foolish Court Jester wants the kingdom to *lighten up* and have some *fun.*

To accept a player, you must go to the heart of the matter. Instead of waiting until you understand a particular actor, create a safe space on the stage so the actor can discover what makes its heart sing.

Acceptance gives a wonderful serenity, a great moral strength and a deep sense of peace.
ROBERTO ASSAGIOLI

Accepting an Actor

Return to the inner theatre and see your actor on stage—the actor you recognized in step one. As director, assure the actor that you are here to accept it and to understand its heart's desire. (If the Judge appears and attempts to influence you, ask it to return to its chamber.)

To discover what the actor feels and wants from the inside out, imagine stepping into its shoes. Then move back and forth between the actor and yourself as director until your actor says, "Ah ha! That's what I really want."

✍ *Create the following script with your actor.*

DIRECTOR: What are you feeling?
ACTOR: I'm feeling . . .
DIRECTOR: What is missing for you?
ACTOR: The thing that is missing is . . .
DIRECTOR: What do you really want?
ACTOR: What I really want is **. . .**
DIRECTOR: If you had that, what would you want even more?
ACTOR: What I would want even more is . . .
DIRECTOR: If you had that, is there something even more important? What is your heart's deepest desire?
ACTOR: The thing that would make my heart sing is . . .
DIRECTOR: I have good news. First of all, I am here to give you all the love and support you need. You are not alone. Second, what you have been looking for is already inside. This is the quality you must express to become a star.
ACTOR: Hmm . . . What I have been looking for is already inside of me? To become a star, I need to bring forth the quality of . . .
DIRECTOR: Now we both know the truth behind your mask. What is it like to know that this quality is already within you?
ACTOR: In this moment I feel . . .
DIRECTOR: When you are [name the star quality here] as a natural way of being in the world, how are things different?
ACTOR: One thing that is different is . . .

*If you love it enough
anything will
talk to you.*
GEORGE W. CARVER

*Our highest calling in life
is precisely to take loving
care of ourselves.*
ERICH FROMM

DIRECTOR: How does already being [the star quality] transform the old play? Take time to relive the old scene knowing what you perceive now. How can you create a new ending for that scene?

─────◆─────

Anna's Second Step in Directing

Remember Anna's actor, Stressman? Watch to see how Anna now moves through the second step of directing.

DIRECTOR: What are you feeling?

ACTOR: I'm feeling overwhelmed—tired and exhausted.

DIRECTOR: What is missing for you?

ACTOR: The thing that's missing is time to rest, relax, and have opportunities for pleasure.

DIRECTOR: What do you really want?

ACTOR: What I really want is time for breaks. I want to do things with less effort. I want to be aware of the pleasure in what I'm doing. I want to use time instead of chasing after time.

DIRECTOR: If you already had more time for breaks and pleasure, what would you want that is even more important?

ACTOR: Hmm . . . What I would want even more would be to relax and *just be.*

DIRECTOR: If you had the time for relaxing and just being, is there something even more you'd like? What's your heart's *deepest* desire?

ACTOR: Well . . . if I were already relaxed and just being, I'd feel *joy*! Yes, *that's it*! My heart's deepest desire is to *feel the joy in just being*! . . . I never knew this is what I'd discover. [laughing]

DIRECTOR: I have good news. First of all, I am here to give you all the love and support and time and joy you want. I understand your need to *just be* instead of working all the time. Second, what you have been looking for is already inside. *Joy* is the quality you can now just naturally express to become a star.

ACTOR: Yes, that's it. I can relax and simply bring forth the quality of joy to be my star self!

To love oneself is the beginning of a life-long romance.
OSCAR WILDE

DIRECTOR: Now we both know the truth behind your mask. What is it like to already be joyful in this moment?

ACTOR: In this moment I feel wonderful. I feel recognized as who I really am. I look around with fresh eyes and feel as though I can see new possibilities for bringing forth my true role in the play. How wonderful to know what I have to give and that I have the space to bring it into being. Thank you very much for giving me the opportunity to be on stage and to be listened to. Now my *real name* is Joy.

The last time I saw him, he was walking down Lover's lane holding his own hand.
FRED ALLEN

Notice how Anna, in working with Stressman, refused to be sidetracked by his first five or six statements; how she gently yet relentlessly said, in effect, "I'm not going to go away or give up until we've swept aside a few of these masks and the paint jobs on the masks. I am going to stay here and assist you untiringly in peeling the layers away." This made it safe for Stressman to keep going deeper inside until he found the pot of gold in his heart. *Joy!* He found the joy of pure being without having to *perform* any longer. Suddenly he realized that he was really Joy instead of Stressman. What a radical change this actor is making! But that's not the end. Anna will soon take still another step in directing—a third step. There's more to come!

Character Assassination

You may wonder what happens if you don't accept a particular actor. (Meaning: What if you reject a part of yourself?) Is it ever okay to send an actor into exile, or to fire one, or to lock one in the dungeon, or even to kill one if it happens to be a despicable villain?

Regardless of how ugly, monstrous, or vile certain parts of us may be, we can't destroy our actors. *Why?* Because they (we) are patterns of energy and *we can't destroy energy*. Energy can only be *transmuted* or *transformed*.

Let me explain it this way. Just as a piano has many keys, you have many actors. Each actor represents a special note or *tone* of your being. If you deny or try to get rid of an actor, it's the same as disabling one of those keys. You lose your capacity to play and hear that particular note, to know that inner quality. Consequently, you also become insensitive or intolerant of that attribute in other people. If you cut off or fire your actors, you end up with a very limited troupe.

Fired or banished actors may be shoved out of sight but they're not out of mind. *What we resist, persists.* If sent away, an actor will leave the scene temporarily, but will return after it has established an underground resistance movement. In other words, it gets bigger, not better.

Earlier, I told the tale of Mack and his *bad-ass ringleaders.* If he had not brought them into the spotlight, you can be certain they'd have sabotaged his studies in school. As it was, he sat down to talk with them and, in listening, discovered that they were all afraid of being dumped or killed. He assured them that he wouldn't hurt them. He assured them that he needed their help.

Although not totally convinced that Mack would be a good director, they began to think he *might* take them seriously instead of annihilating them. Maybe Mack would listen as he promised. They decided to give him a chance. So:

Elly said she'd help him with his studies if he made sure playboy-Floyd didn't come on to her. She didn't like being treated like a whore. She also wanted new nylons.

Fat Albert said he'd cooperate if Mack would take time off from his studies to jog with him.

Rogues in a crowd, single each other out.
ANONYMOUS

Clyde (the Hell's Angel) told Mack to quit talking about going to school and just do it. He said he wouldn't get in the way, but he wouldn't help either.

Izzy said going back to school could be an opportunity for him to use more creative insight and less sneakiness. He'd rather be *cunning* than *sneaky* anyway.

Floyd was embarrassed about the idea of school, but told Mack to go ahead and have fun. He said he'd wait outside, and if Mack dropped out of school, he'd be right there.

Obviously, director Mack had more work to do with his actors, but at least he was now creating a safe place for them to participate. I reminded Mack that *it takes only one bad actor to ruin the whole show, while it takes all the actors working together to produce a successful performance.*

Initially Mack's actors were afraid of being assassinated. (The fear of dying lies at the bottom of all our other fears.) Indeed, I have known people who tried to kill their parts, but it doesn't work. It just creates terror, and then more terror. When you feel like getting rid of a part of yourself, you must ask, "Who is killing whom?" If you give permission to your inner Murderer to destroy another actor, it doesn't create a feeling of safety for the rest of the cast. It simply doesn't solve the problem. (It doesn't work in the inner theatre *or* the outer theatre.)

Killing never resolves a conflict. It just intensifies the fear. Swiss analyst Carl Jung once said, "Every part of the personality we do not love will become hostile to us." If you don't accept an actor, you block your flow of love, and the congested energy creates mental, emotional, and physical distress. When you carry hostility or hatred over a period of time, it can cause dis-ease and eventually destroy your physical body. It's a slow death, but even so, your soul lives on. The playwright doesn't die even if the show turns out to be a tragedy.

But what about an actor who is suicidal?

I am thinking of Lisa, an overweight medical transcriber, who came to me for therapy because her suicidal actor felt so hopeless that she threatened to close the curtain for good. After helping Lisa recognize her suicidal feelings in the form of an actor and listening to what this actor *really* wanted (love), I worked with her as we explored what old

*When one person hates another, it is the hater who falls ill.
When he loves, it is he who becomes whole.
Hatred kills. Love heals.*
BUDDHA

way of acting needed to change. I asked her: what old script is no longer working?

A suicidal actor mistakenly believes it has to die in order to relieve the pain. The deeper truth is that an old script needs to change, because it isn't working any longer. Instead of being allowed to kill itself, the suicidal player needs help in finding a new script and, in doing so, discovering the star quality hidden in its heart. *Not to give expression to one's potential and not to fulfill one's purpose is the real tragedy in life.*

I have no inclination to assault myself; it would be of no use. You may do it if you choose—I refuse.
LEO TOLSTOY

Prominent Broadway actress, director, and acting teacher Uta Hagen emphasizes the importance of admitting to all emotions in the human repertoire. In her book *Respect for Acting* she writes, "We must learn to understand and accept the facets of ourselves which we don't wish to recognize—shyness, selfishness, greed, envy, panic, lack of control, stupidity, etc. and, in admitting to them, enlarge our capacity for identification."

As human beings, we want to be able to express every possible feeling. We want to have all the notes of our emotional potential available. Then whether or not we express certain feelings becomes a matter of choice.

Actors want to be understood and accepted. Your important task as director is to welcome home those you have abandoned, include those who feel lonely, and embrace those who are starved for affection. Every player wants to feel as though he or she is an important member of the cast. Everyone wants to belong!

Third Step in Directing

AS DIRECTOR, I TAKE RESPONSIBILITY FOR MY ACTORS
AND DEVELOP THEIR STAR QUALITIES.

THIRD STEP INVOLVES:
Responsibility
Motivation
Direction
Purpose
Power
Action
Body
Skill
Will

*You don't get to choose
whether you're going to
be responsible. You get to
decide when, not if.*
LAZARIS

Each of us is responsible for staging and producing the pageant of our lives. Once our minds and hearts become involved in directing, we're no longer willing to hand our show over to someone else or to allow an actor to take our place. We welcome the opportunity to take charge of the cast and to orchestrate our daily production.

As director, you'll soon discover that taking charge requires more than *knowing* your selves and *loving* your selves. It also requires *empowering* your selves. The art of directing involves awareness, acceptance, and *action.* The synergy, or combined effort, of these three ultimately leads to self-mastery.

In the third and final step of directing, you learn to take full responsibility for your players and give them a unified sense of purpose and direction. You support their unfolding potential and empower them in new, authentic methods of acting. Empowerment means giving yourself permission to choose and to act. Ultimately, no one can choose for you. No one can take responsibility for you. Orchestrating your life is up to you.

Personal *will* is the dynamic force that initiates action—the power that gets things done in the world. Without will, you would have no energy to move about on the stage. Without will, you would have no power to manifest your dreams. Without will, you would have no purpose in performing.

Many people aren't clear about the meanings of words associated with *power*. To make sure we're all talking about the same thing, I've defined the words I'm using in this third step:

WILL: The capacity to choose and direct one's actions and destiny.
POWER: The ability to act. One's energy or animating force.
EMPOWERMENT: Giving oneself permission to act.
CHOICE: Conscious or unconscious selection of action.
RESPONSIBILITY: The ability to respond.
CONTROL: Using one's will to dominate or coerce another.

Whose Will Is in Charge?

Who *really* is in charge of your show? Is the director in charge, or one of the actors?

What the director wants and what the actors want may be quite different. You may think you want to lose weight, quit smoking, or make a good sales pitch, but then you eat two servings of buttered potatoes, buy another pack of cigarettes, or accidentally forget to call a new customer.

You intend to do what's good for you, but then you don't follow through. Why? Who's sabotaging the show? Well, look around. You'll find one of your actors giving orders.

In the inner theatre, each member of the entourage has a will of its own, which is why you often feel pulled in many directions. Your will varies with whomever you're identified at a particular time—the playwright, the director, or one of your actors.

How can we tell whose will is in charge?

To begin with, the *playwright's will* is effortless and infinitely powerful. It is your "soul-power" or *spiritual* will. Like the sun, its presence is energizing and life-giving. When you're aligned with your playwright's will, the show unfolds naturally and you trust that life is as it should be. You *allow* and *flow* with what *is*, and your play inspires and benefits all those around you.

The *director's will* represents personal power—the ability to move and create on Earth. It is the central organizing power of the personality. As director, when you're using the life force, you are centered, impartial, and empowering. Your power is skillful (intelligent), good (loving), and strong.

Occasionally, movie stars will describe what it's like to work with good directors. In a *St. Louis Post-Dispatch* interview, Tom Cruise, a star in *A Few Good Men,* spoke of his experience with director Rob Reiner. "Rob's a big guy physically, and there's a sweetness about him that catches you. You bounce back and forth with this guy. He loves actors. He loves what he's doing. . . . He's a guy who wants, almost wills, his actors to be great."

"Willing actors to be great" is a sign of an accomplished director. When actors feel understood, accepted, and supported, they realize that

PLAYWRIGHT'S WILL
spiritual power
spiritual purpose
infinite dynamism
organizing power
totally free
effortless
peaceful

⊙

DIRECTOR'S WILL
personal power
directive
strong/good/skillful
empowering
responsive

⊙

ACTOR'S WILL
(ACCOMPLISHED)
competent
efficient
courageous
capable
disciplined
decisive
persistent
effective
determined

⊙

(UNACCOMPLISHED)
dominating
intimidating
rebellious
stubborn
procrastinating
impotent
fearful
helpless
cruel

the director is there for *them*. Then working together for the common goal is easy.

What about the *actor's will*? You'll discover that actors express all the polarities and nuances of power, be it good or bad, strong or weak, hurtful or harmless. When used wisely, their power is constructive. When not balanced with intelligence and love, their power is destructive.

Strong, Good, and Skillful Will

In his book *The Act of Will*, Roberto Assagioli explains that the aspects of the fully developed will are *strong will*, *skillful will*, and *good will*. Let's look more closely at these three aspects.

Strength does not come from physical capacity. It comes from an indomitable will.
MAHATMA GANDHI

STRONG WILL is the dynamic power—the fire—of the self. With strong will, you have the energy (the fuel) to act. You have the power to do what you want to do, and no one can persuade you to veer from your intention.

GOOD WILL is the intention to act in ways that unite and heal. With good will, you value the life force in all living beings and preserve the integrity of relationships. You see the good in others and respond with compassion. You desire to do no harm.

Nothing is so strong as gentleness; nothing so gentle as real strength.
FRANCIS DE SALES

SKILLFUL WILL is intelligent and wise action based on an understanding of principles. With skillful will, you develop the most effective strategy to achieve what you want . . . when you want it . . . in the most direct way . . . with the least amount of effort.

When these three aspects of will are not developed and balanced, you'll discover all the human behaviors that cause pain and suffering. Have you noticed how Tyrants use strong and sometimes skillful will, but lack good will? Have you seen how a codependent Lover has plenty of good will, but lacks skillful will in setting boundaries or the strong will to maintain them? Have you observed how the Manipulator is very clever (skillful) in getting you to do *his* will, for *his* own purposes, with little regard for *you*? Where is the love here?

Each person has the responsibility to develop will and to learn how to use power wisely! So, *how does the director use power with the actors? What does the correct use of will look like?* One thing is certain: in using power, the wise and caring director is not a *dictator*, but rather is an advocate, supporter, midwife, or evocateur. Once an actor is recognized and accepted, once it is listened to and embraced, it doesn't need to be pushed, forced, or manhandled. As we saw at the end of the second step, the actor is *already* eager and willing to work together with the director. The actor *wants* to develop a new script and work out the details of becoming a more skillful actor.

If the actor still feels resistant, the director needs to return to step two and come into resonance with what the actor wants at a deeper level. Only when you have done so will the actor be willing to redirect its energies and create a new script.

After you help an actor define what makes its heart sing, your next step is simply to stand by that actor and create the space for its star quality to emerge. Your task is to allow the actor to get in touch with *the way life wants to flow* through him or through her. Isn't this beautiful? By giving the actor permission to express what is deep inside, you are empowering that actor, that part of you, to act authentically. As director, your task is truly *effortless*.

✍ *Which aspect of the will is most developed in your life? Which is least developed? Explain.*

Before taking action,
ask three questions:
Is it skillful?
Is it good for all?
*Will it empower others
and myself?*

Inner Freedom

Ah freedom! In the inner theatre, you are free to make your own choices and decisions. Free to follow your own path, your own light, your own inner aspirations. You are even free to make *mistakes.*

However, with freedom comes responsibility. *Free will does not give us permission to impose our will upon others!* Free will does not give us license to abuse others, damage property, or pollute the environment. Imposing our will, or compelling others to conform to our desires, is a violation of power.

True freedom comes when you make a commitment to take charge of your life and to do so in a way that is skillful, loving, and powerful. These are not just nice words or concepts. What I'm talking about here will ultimately determine whether your life's play is successful or not. Success depends on your *total commitment* to taking responsibility for your production. If you want to be effective, if you want to feel strength rising from the depths of your being, you have to use your will—your power! There is no freedom where there is no power.

How do you develop your will? How do you empower yourself? You begin by giving yourself permission to make your own choices and decisions. You must know *without a doubt* that *you* are in charge of your life. When others make decisions for you, you give up your power *and* your freedom. You relinquish your will and you feel weak and ineffective. Having a wishy-washy will results in a wishy-washy melodrama.

Choosing and making decisions is not something new. In fact, you do this all the time, but generally you're not aware of what you're doing. Now it's time to be conscious of your choices and to use your will with awareness. This is actually fun. No kidding!

I'll tell you how to maximize both your freedom and your power. Begin by asking yourself two important questions: *What am I willing to do? What am I not willing to do?* When you say "yes" to something, you indicate that you are willing to take an action. When you say "no," you indicate that you are not willing to act. If you don't want to do something and you hold back from doing it, pay attention to that feeling. *Resistance* gives you important information. Your reluctance to do something—be it giving someone a back rub, washing the car,

When you give your power to someone else, you inevitably lose some of your power.
PAMELA ZIEMANN

serving on a new committee, or visiting your ailing parents—is an indication that your will is saying "no." If you force yourself to act despite your resistance, you'll set up an inner conflict. "Do it!" "I don't want to." "Do it anyway." "No." Then you feel frustrated, resentful, or obligated. The inner conflict splits your will and you lose power.

How much more elegant it is to stop and ask: "What am I not willing to do?" (my "no") Then follow with the next question: "What am I willing to do instead?" This is the "yes" behind your "no." This is where the fun comes in. Determine what you *are willing* to do instead. You might say, "I'm not willing to give you a backrub tonight, but I am willing to lie beside you and talk softly." Or, "I'm not willing to wash the car now, but I am willing to wash it on Saturday." Or, "I don't want to serve on the new committee, but I am willing to find someone else to serve." Or, "I'm not willing to give up my Sunday afternoon to visit the folks, but I would be willing to hire a taxi to bring them here for the afternoon. They could watch the football game with us."

Here's another example: Pam, a busy student and secretary, was in a bad mood over the upcoming Christmas holidays. She didn't want to go through the bother of holiday planning. Pam asked her disgruntled part, whom she called Ms. Scrooge, to list what she was *not willing to do* (her "no"). Immediately Ms. Scrooge listed ten things other people were expecting from her. Then Pam asked what she *was willing to do* instead (her "yes"). Ms. Scrooge's face lit up and she quickly enumerated three things she *wanted* to do for the holidays.

This was an easy way to bring Pam's resistance out into the open. If Ms. Scrooge had been left in the shadows, she would have dampened Pam's holiday spirit, perhaps even spoiling the whole season. As it was, Pam gave herself permission to do only those things on her "yes" list, and she ended up enjoying the holidays.

Begin to honor your will now by experimenting with your "yes" and "no." See for yourself how power flows through you when your will is clear and you give yourself permission to act upon your "yes." Notice how your life begins to change for the better. *Ah, yes. Freedom!*

✍ *What present life situation is creating a problem for you? What are you not willing to do (your "no")? What are you willing to do instead (your "yes")?*

I don't want to hear what a player can't do, I want to hear what he can do.
RICK PATINA
BASKETBALL COACH

Power and Glory

Distinguished Bulgarian philosopher and spiritual master Omraam Mikhaël Aïvanhov says: "True power does not lie in ordering other people about or in abusing or punishing them or putting them to death. True power lies in warming them to the point where they can no longer resist and have to undress . . . where they cast off the heavy, dark layers under which they are hiding."

He goes on to explain that the power of love is like the sun that shines on persons and warms them so they *want* to change. This is the kind of power ideally used by the inner director. In this presence, actors *want* to take off their protective shields, swords, bulletproof vests, and helmets. They *want* to walk barefoot in the grass, feel the sun on their face, and hear the birds singing.

Mahatma Gandhi called this power "soul-force." Gandhi, of course, was the Indian lawyer, writer, and spiritual master who freed India from British foreign rule without firing a shot. He demonstrated the principles of nonviolence or *Satyagraha*—the spiritual force born of truth and love.

Gandhi did not view an adversary as an enemy to be overcome, but as "a participant in the search for a truthful solution to the conflict." He believed it was important never to use force to win a cause, since in the long run doing so doesn't work. He also believed it was important never to yield to the force someone else tries to exert over you. To his exploiters he would say: "We will not submit to injustice—not merely because it is destroying us, but because it is destroying you as well."

Gandhi believed that beneath the masks we all wear is the glory of our real self, which is completely fearless, joyful, and unconditionally loving. By taking off his own mask, Gandhi eliminated hostility and fear from his personality, thereby modeling the use of true power for the rest of us.

Ways to Use Power

We are learning to use power in constructive ways, but often we fail. Consider how you use power and how you respond to others' use of power by examining the following two lists. The first indicates ways we use power when we are afraid; the second indicates ways we use power when we are loving.

When we are afraid . . .
  We struggle in the battleground of life.
  Our goal is survival.
  We use Outer Sight.
  We defend ourselves to keep control.
  We use weapons to overpower.
  We manipulate and force our way.
  We see others as enemies.
  We feel angry and disconnected.
  We are suspicious of the unknown.
  We want to hurt or kill the enemy.
  We change things by destroying.
  We possess.
  We exclude and constrict.
  We want to win battles.
  We scratch, fight, punish, hurt, or kill.
  Our show is a bloody drama.
  We create melodramas and tragedies.
  Everyone loses.

When we are loving . . .
  We enjoy the landscape of life.
  Our goal is to excel.
  We use Inner Sight.
  We engage others to share power.
  We use intelligence to empower.
  We generate win-win options.
  We see others as friends.
  We feel courageous and united.
  We are curious about the unknown.
  We want to befriend strangers.
  We change things by transforming.
  We share.
  We include and expand.

*In violence we forget
who we are.*
MARY MCCARTHY

*You cannot shake hands
with a clenched fist.*
GOLDA MEIR

*In the face of the sublime
the savage flees.*
ROBERTO ASSAGIOLI

We want to resolve conflicts.
We talk, disarm, and stand steady.
Our show is a spontaneous play.
We create adventures and comedies.
Everyone wins.

✍ *Write a description of the way you generally use power.*

Control Dramas

The conflict that arises from a clash of wills is called a *control drama*. Since this is what most of our movies and television shows are about, it's no secret that these dramas make great entertainment. In our personal lives, however, control dramas aren't much fun. Dramatic, yes. Fun, no! When people with power collide, there's always trouble, and often violence.

You know you're involved in a control drama when you experience intimidation, force, abuse, manipulation, victimization, fear, or anger. Sometimes you're the one forcing your will, and sometimes you're the one being forced. You know both sides of the coin. We all do, because we're human.

Forcing our will is an act of violence. Violence in any form is a sure sign that strong will is dominating the heart and the head. Without compassion and sensibility, the will turns evil and destructive

We experience control dramas with other people and within ourselves. Inner actors often fight among themselves, and some even defy you, the director. This is where *self-control* comes in, meaning *you* taking responsibility for the behavior of your players.

Actors who are impulsive, abusive, or criminal need to be *restrained until retrained*. As directors, we must help our actors learn to control their impulses. We can't allow our actors to hurt each other or other people. It's simply *not* okay for Boozer Bob to drive while intoxicated, for tired Teacher to insult a student, for impatient Wife to berate her husband, or for Tyrant Father to whip a child (the inner or outer child).

Talk about whipping. I am reminded of Charles, a middle-aged sales executive, whose story demonstrates how violence breeds more violence. Charles came to therapy to discover what the boils on his back were trying to tell him. He knew the symptoms had a message, but he didn't know what they were trying to convey. To discover the message, Charles imagined what the boils would say if they could talk. To his surprise, the boils said they were "boiling mad." In Charles'

Fear is the parent of Cruelty.
FROUDE

I was looking outside myself for strength and confidence but it comes from within. It is there all the time.
ANNA FREUD

mind, the boils immediately transformed into a prisoner chained to the wall of a cell. The prisoner was mad enough to kill.

Upset with the image, Charles asked me if he should, using the power of his imagination, let the prisoner go. But even the thought terrified him. I suggested that releasing the prisoner would be dangerous until Charles, as director, discovered more about the prisoner. *Why was he here? What had he done? What did he need?*

Gathering courage, Charles agreed to talk to the chained actor.

The prisoner confessed that he was chained in the dungeon for wanting to kill his father. Instantly, Charles knew what it meant. As an adolescent, Charles' father had beat him mercilessly, and the youngster vowed he would get revenge when he grew up. The chains, evidence of his own self-restraint, kept him from executing his plan, but they didn't stop the rage.

Charles now realized that the time had come to deal with the hatred he had toward his father. He told the prisoner that he was ready to do something about the pain and boiling rage. He was willing to help the tormented part find a safe way to express these deep feelings, but he knew he needed my support as a therapist. Charles also knew the days ahead would be difficult, but he said, "This is what I have to do in order to be free, otherwise I'll die in the prison of my own hatred."

I've often wondered what happened to Charles. He canceled the next session, stating that he was waiting on some money and that he'd call to reschedule when the money came. He never called. I tried contacting him, but to no avail. I've prayed for him—that in time, in some way, he would have help in forgiving his father and in releasing his inner Prisoner.

The control drama between Charles and his father was more extreme than that of most people, yet we all have experienced the violation of our will to some degree and we all know how bad it feels. Furthermore, we all have violated the will of others. We know how that feels as well.

In playing out power struggles, there are three ways we can use our power or "might":

Anger sharpens kitchen knives at the local supermarket . . . His face is scarred from adolescent battles.

J. RUTH GENDLER

Fight-might: fighting to get our own way.

Flight-might: giving up power and running away.

Right-might: standing steady and thinking of the most skillful, loving, and powerful way to handle a situation.

Both *fight-might* and *flight-might* end in suffering and sometimes tragedy. *Right-might* is the only way that holds the promise for resolution.

Control Drama Inventory

✍ *Consider the control dramas you've been involved in and answer the following questions on paper:*

Recall a time when you controlled another person. What happened? What did you do? What did the other person do?

What feelings did you have? What did you want?

What were you not willing to do? (Your "no")

What would you have been willing to do instead? (Your "yes")

Was the conflict resolved? If so, how? If not, why not?

Recall a time when another person controlled you. What happened? What did you do? What did the other person do?

What feelings did you have? What did you want?

What were you not willing to do? (Your "no")

What would you have been willing to do instead? (Your "yes")

Was the conflict resolved? If so, how? If not, why not?

Anger is our friend. Not a nice friend. But a very, very loyal friend. It will always tell us when we have been betrayed. It will always tell us when we have betrayed ourselves.
JULIA CAMERON

The Old Script

Like people, characters hang onto old scripts and continue with their soap operas until they are offered better parts. Makes perfect sense, doesn't it? What movie star would pass up a role in a classic production to continue in a second-rate skin flick. Actors love it when someone recognizes their potential and invites them to become part of a show with richer substance.

Our daily dramas give us clues as to which actors need new scripts. In the movie *New York Stories: Oedipus Wrecks*, Woody Allen plays the part of a fifty-year-old lawyer who has unresolved feelings toward his mother. The melodrama between the two goes on year after year. Angst. Guilt. Entrapment.

Then one day, Woody and his girlfriend take his mother to a magic show. The magician, looking over the audience, selects the mother to participate in his disappearing act. Complaining and fidgeting with her purse, she steps into the Magic Box and . . . disappears. But then, something goes terribly wrong. The magician can't bring her back. She mysteriously and peacefully vanishes.

It's a horrible, wonderful mystery. She's gone and it's not even Woody's fault. His lifetime problem has just evaporated and now he's free! He believes the problem with his mother is finally over, but it's not. To his consternation, her face appears in the sky in the middle of a busy New York intersection. Larger than life, she broadcasts intimate details of his life to the throngs below. Feeling abject humiliation, he is now unable to go anywhere to escape her insufferable, intrusive presence.

Like Woody, we learn to play certain roles in the Family Theatre from the beginning of our lives. Unconsciously, we take on a script (life plan) that provides us with personal identity and purpose.

In the beginning, the script gives meaning to our performance and is often based on the need to be loved or on the need to survive. While the assumptions we make early in life may be appropriate for Children's Theatre, they are seldom valid for Adult Theatre. In fact, if our childhood script isn't edited or revised, we may reenact the old themes until we die.

Those who do not have power over the story that dominates their lives, power to retell it, to re-think it, deconstruct it, joke about it, and change it as times change, truly are powerless because they cannot think new thoughts.
SALMAN RUSHDIE

The playwright, however, continually presents us with new situations, which give us the opportunity to change our method of acting. Given new opportunities, we are pushed and pulled between two points of tension. The first comes from a part that resists change, and the second comes from a part that knows more is possible. The struggle is between the past (who we've been) and destiny (who we can be). If the conflict is resolved, we experience the ecstasy of knowing we are on the right path; if it is not, we experience more confusion and frustration.

The actor who is stuck in an old role resists change, not because it is "bad," but because it doesn't know a better way. Often this actor demands center stage and calls attention to itself out of distress. It mechanically replays the same unsuccessful scenes over and over. Take Woody, for example. In the movie, his old girlfriend leaves him and he finds a *new* girlfriend, one who relates to him a lot like his mother. We are almost sure that the old script will continue to be enacted and that Woody will experience more of the same old feelings of angst, guilt, and entrapment.

The problem must be resolved on the inner stage. This is an inner thing. To resolve his problem, Woody needs to step into his director's chair and help his inner Son and inner Mother rewrite their scripts. Since the inner world is alive and fluid, old scripts can be edited and new scripts can be created. The inner Child can be loved by the Mother he's always wanted, and the inner Mother can have the respect from her inner Son that she wants.

By letting go of old scripts and removing old masks, we allow what's alive, fresh, and new to emerge. Yes, the dictatorial Manager can relax and become a creative leader. The deceitful Lawyer can become a true advocate for justice. The Supermom can kick off her shoes and release the expectations she puts on herself to be all things to all people. There is a way to change.

Whatever is in your childhood you will find repeating itself in your life, until you embrace it.
PTAAH

Enacting our soul means creating a fresh self, an ever-changing yet enduring self, that can play any role, take any position—with full awareness and control.
GABRIELLE ROTH

A New Script

When an old script no longer serves a purpose, that means the time has come to weave new themes into our narratives and re-vision our future.

The movement from letting go of an old script to inventing a new one can be perceived as a three-act play. For example, Dante's *Divine Comedy* demonstrates the progression beautifully. In the first act, Dante finds himself in a dark forest and is in total despair. The old way is simply not working. Then along comes Virgil (a Latin poet representing human discernment), who leads him in the descent into Hell—the exploration of the subconscious.

The second act tells of their ascending the mountain of Purgatory, where Dante experiences moral refinement and an expansion of consciousness. At this point Virgil disappears, because human reason has accomplished its function and cannot go further. Now, in the third act, Beatrice (Divine Wisdom) becomes Dante's guide, for she is capable of leading him into Paradise—the exploration of the superconscious. It is here that Dante catches a vision of what's possible.

The tension between your struggling actor and Destiny can be resolved by taking the actor on a journey into the past to discover the origins of its outmoded script (which you did in the first step of directing, when you asked your actor what caused its suffering). To create the new script, you must remember what your actor wants in the bottom of its heart (which you discovered in the second step). Then you take your actor into the future to discover the possibilities for who it may become (which you will do in the third step).

The third step of directing involves creating the space for *what is already inside* to be developed and expressed. You'll want to give your actor the space it needs to unfold and to express its star quality. You don't have to *do* anything to make it happen. You just have to create the space.

I once read that Isadora Duncan, the famous American dancer, would place her hand on her solar plexus and stand unmoving until she felt the origin of movement, or "music of the soul," rising from within her. When she felt this energy, she allowed it to flow through her body, "filling it with vibrating light," then she would dance. Or you could say *she became the dance.*

The director's task is to believe there is something inside that wants to flow up and out. You must know beyond a doubt that the soul has something to express through this particular role at this particular time. Given the opportunity, the soul will move through this actor to express an exquisite quality in a totally unique way—your way

As director, you don't have to push, shove, bully, force, coerce, or *try to make* your actor become a star. *Your task is effortless.* Your actor will naturally develop its potential as you clear the stage for its performance. The star-seed has already been planted. Give it room to grow. The player's purpose is to become who he or she is meant to be.

Each actor is a part of the unfolding mystery of who you are. To practice changing a script, call back the actor with whom you have been working. Take the third step in directing and assist the actor in developing its inherent star quality.

I've never sought success in order to get fame and money; it's the talent and the passion that count in success.
INGRID BERGMAN

Directing an Actor

Sit back in your director's chair and call your actor to the stage. Thank the actor for being patient while you've been learning the steps of directing. Now you're ready to help this actor become the best it can be.

✍ *Together, co-create a new script filled with passion and purpose.*

Want a bigger harvest? Plant more seeds. Expect more and ask for more.
JOHN 10:10

DIRECTOR: What old script is no longer working?
ACTOR:
DIRECTOR: What are you no longer willing to do? (Your "no")
ACTOR: I'm no longer willing to . . .
DIRECTOR: If assured of success, what would you love to do? (Your "yes")
ACTOR: What I would love to do is . . .
DIRECTOR: What resources, props, or funds could help you play your part most effectively? (Be specific)
ACTOR:
DIRECTOR: Who in the supporting cast could help you be successful?
ACTOR:

*If the solution is not
beautiful, I know
it is wrong.*
BUCKMINSTER FULLER

DIRECTOR: Let's ask the playwright how your script could be even better.

PLAYWRIGHT: [As the playwright, write a letter to your director and actor and give your perspective.]

DIRECTOR: [To actor] Considering all this, how can your new role benefit the rest of the cast and other people?

ACTOR:

DIRECTOR: What is the name of this new play?

ACTOR:

DIRECTOR: What specific actions are you willing to take to bring this about?

ACTOR:

*Every noble work is at
first impossible.*
THOMAS CARLYLE

DIRECTOR: Congratulations! Good work! We're going to bring this about together with little effort. Before long, you'll look back and realize that you have already accomplished this, and that you're truly an accomplished star!

ACTOR: You've been a great director! Thanks so much for learning how to direct me.

Anna's Third Step in Directing

Anna's actor, Stressman, now called "Joy," was eager to be led through this third and final step in directing:

*Shoot for the moon. Even
if you miss it you will land
among the stars.*
LES BROWN

DIRECTOR: I see there is an imbalance between working with effort and simply releasing. You haven't known how to make work easier and more enjoyable. Now, Joy, what are you no longer willing to do? What is your "no"?

ACTOR: I am no longer willing to push everyone forward, warning that there is not enough time. I am no longer willing to emphasize the importance of being serious and working hard. I am not willing to work up to exhaustion, always looking for how things can be done even more perfectly.

DIRECTOR: If assured of success, what would you really love to do? What is your "yes"?

ACTOR: I would love to bring pleasure into the play. I would love to point out the enjoyable moments and give them a larger space. I would like to color the whole play with joy so it radiates more vividness. I am willing to take breaks and relax.

DIRECTOR: To achieve this, what resources might be helpful to you?

ACTOR: I really don't need any material possessions or props. However, anything that has to do with expressing beauty would be helpful. I would like to be in nature and with animals. I'd like to decorate my place with plants and stones. I'd like to incorporate poems, artwork, music, and dancing . . . all of this would help me feel more relaxed and joyful.

DIRECTOR: Who in the supporting cast could help you achieve this?

ACTOR: My American and German friends with whom I share the same kind of humor and laughter.

DIRECTOR: [to her playwright, who is named Augusta.] What suggestion do you have to make the play even better?

(At this point, Anna imagined that she was her wise, loving, powerful playwright, listening to the discussion between herself as director and her actor. After sitting quietly for a few moments to gain a larger perspective, Anna imagined what she would say if she were her soul speaking.)

[Letter from Augusta]

Dear Anna, during the last two days you have discovered that deep in this part of you is the quality of joy. And now you ask me for help to make this role even better. With your humor, your sense of beauty, your love of nature, and your sensitivity to others, you have a large field to realize this quality in life and in the world.

Dear Joy, I understand your concerns about limits and the feeling of not being capable of playing this role more effectively. I suggest that you depend on your close partner, Creativity. In this relationship, you can easily find ways of relaxing and having a wonderful play in life. What's more, every time you ask me, you'll get the next segment of the new

*Life ideals are lifelike
portraits seen in advance.*
DAVID SWING

script. I am here to inspire you from moment to moment. I enjoy living with you all the time and forever.

Your playwright, Augusta

DIRECTOR: Thank you, Augusta. Just knowing you're always here helps a lot. [to Joy] Joy, how would playing this new script benefit the rest of the cast and the other people in our life?

ACTOR: My new role would make everyone's acting more enjoyable. They would see the play with brighter-colored glasses and the rehearsals would be fun. Other people would enjoy being around us and they would smile and laugh much more.

DIRECTOR: What could be the name of this new performance?

ACTOR: *The Joy of Life.*

DIRECTOR: What specific actions are you willing to take to bring this about?

ACTOR: The thing I can do to make this a reality is to take short breaks during the day, to relax. I can be aware of joyful events and take an active part in them. I can share time with other people in activities such as dancing, singing, and playing. I can look at problems more positively and see how they are part of the bigger play. Yes, even working on problems can be a joyful act!

DIRECTOR: Congratulations! Good work! We're going to bring this about together, and without much effort. Before long, you'll look back and realize that you have already accomplished this and that you're truly an accomplished star!

ACTOR: Thank you, Anna, for being a great director! Working with you in the future will be a joy.

❦

*Go confidently in the
direction of your
dreams! Live the
life you've imagined.*
HENRY DAVID THOREAU

Future Self

We create our play with every thought and feeling we have, from moment to moment. This means that whatever we pay attention to will grow stronger and whatever we withdraw our attention from will grow weaker. Knowing this, we ought not even to look at the old script anymore. It's out of date and it doesn't do justice to who you are today. Tear it up and throw it away. It's finished.

Now, imagine that you have leaped ahead in time—into the future—and the actor you have been working with is already an accomplished star. Bring the future into this moment and experience it as real *now*. (It really is anyway!)

✍ *What is it like to express your star quality in daily life? As the actor, write a letter to a friend telling how you are living this new script. Tell how it all came to happen. Be specific.*

Summary of the Steps in Directing

Recognize

Consider the present drama of your life and pay attention to a particular role or part you play. Envision this part as an actor on stage and, together with that actor, develop a character profile by having it answer these general questions about itself ("you" below refers to the actor):

> *What do you look like?*
> *How do you act?*
> *What do you feel?*
> *What do you think?*
> *What do you say?*
> *What happened to cause your suffering?*
> *What is your usual script?*
> *What is your name?*

As director, acknowledge that this actor has something important to contribute.

Accept

With an open heart, create a safe place for your actor. Move back and forth between being director and actor until you come into resonance and "get" what the actor is wanting. Help your actor find answers to the following questions about itself.

> *What are you feeling?*
> *What is missing for you?*
> *What do you need or want?*
> *If you had that, what would you want even more?*
> *And if you had that, what would be even more important? What would make your heart sing?*
> *What is it like to know you already have what you want in this moment?*

As director, look with compassion into the actor's heart and acknowledge that what it has been looking for is already present. This is the potential star-quality, waiting to be developed.

Direct

Along with your actor, design a new script that would support your actor in expressing its emerging star-quality. Consult with your playwright and members of the supporting cast to improve the script. How would your actor answer these questions?

What old script is no longer working for you?

What are you no longer willing to do? (Your "no")

If assured of success, what would you love to do? (Your "yes")

What resources or props would be helpful?

Who in the supporting cast could help you become successful?

What suggestions does your playwright have to make your role even better?

How would your revised part benefit the rest of the cast and other people?

What could be the name of this new performance?

What specific actions are you willing to take to bring this about?

As director, assure the actor of your continued presence and express gratitude for its cooperation. Act *as if* the new scenario is already a reality.

Super-Power

In directing your inner characters, where do you get the necessary strength to make changes? What is your source of power?

Generally, we focus so intently on our drama that we forget or deny our most powerful, creative source. Instead of using "soular" energy, we are content to use self-generated, "battery-powered" resources. The first is constant and continuous while the second is limited and exhaustible.

Soul-power is also called the life force, or *chi*. Those who use "soul-force" feel rejuvenated and energized, while those who depend on personal energy often feel tired and depleted. To access your super-power, all you have to do is begin by envisioning *a shaft of light* coming from the Universal Playwright . . . down to your playwright . . . and on down to you as director. Feel yourself bathed in the light. Your playwright serves as a step-down transformer so you'll have the right energy for your work.

Filmmaker Julia Cameron, in her book *The Artist's Way*, calls this switching on "spiritual electricity." Someone has to turn on the switch to start the flow. If we don't do it for ourselves, who will do it for us? To receive illumination, inspiration, and more energy, we must make the first move. When we're in this stream of light, we get amazing ideas. We experience surprising coincidences and delightful epiphanies. We feel confident. We're in the *flow* of life.

You don't have to be afraid that your playwright won't be there when you need help. Since you are absolutely essential to the Earth performance, your playwright won't abandon you. In fact, over time, you'll be amused by all the ingenious ways your playwright invents to communicate with you. The playwright is *always* here, waiting for you to ask for help. Yes, your soul is continually devising ways to get ideas, love, and energy through to you. As you are willing to receive, you shall receive.

Relax and surrender to the will of your playwright, knowing that your playwright wants you to enjoy life to the fullest. And now, to experience your playwright in a more intimate way, find a quiet spot where you won't be distracted and prepare to take a little trip into paradise—the home of your playwright.

Soul force is born of truth and love . . . It is gentle. It never wounds.
GANDHI

Visiting the Playwright

Sit back, relax, and prepare to visit your playwright—your super-power. Allow this experience to be real. It is!

Return to the stage of your theatre, where all is quiet and empty. . . . Take a deep breath, then go backstage . . . enter the right wing . . . and begin to climb the staircase leading to the mysterium.

Stop for a moment and look at yourself in the gold-framed mirrors on each side of the stairs. . . . Light from the upper levels illuminates your profile, creating a soft glow around you.

Quickly and easily climb to the top. Stepping into the mysterium, watch as the ceiling rolls open, revealing the sky. Take a deep breath of the fresh air . . . and now another.

As you look around, notice a fine-grained marble disk about three feet in diameter, inlaid in the floor. The disk is a magical system of teleportation. When you stand on the marble, you can activate a beam of light by focusing your thought and saying "Activate Beam." A beam will then appear and surround you, energizing you with its high frequency. With ease and comfort, it will transport you to the realm of your playwright.

When you're ready, stand on the marble and activate the beam with your thought. . . . Imagine a glimmering shaft of light surrounding you. Sense the light gently suffusing your whole being . . . until every cell is glowing. Your body feels light and spacious. . . . You feel lighthearted and peaceful. . . . Your mind is light and free . . .

Feeling light as a feather, float up the beam . . . up . . . up . . . higher and lighter . . . until you break through a hole in the sky and enter a dreamlike world of light and color. Gently put your feet down on a marble disk like the one in your mysterium, realizing that this one is pure energy.

Adjust your eyes to the shimmering colors all around. This realm may seem strangely familiar. It's similar to beautiful places you've seen before, but here everything is energy. Flashes and streaks of light scintillate all around. A faint glow surrounds everything in the vista.

To reach the place where this Self resides means a climb, an ascent to the heights of the superconscious.
ROBERTO ASSAGIOLI

Mortal I know I am,
short lived; and yet,
whenever I watch
the multitude of
swirling stars, then
I no longer tread
this earth, but rise
to feast with God,
and enjoy the food
of the immortals.
PTOLEMY

The air is clear and fresh. You catch a whiff of a particular flower essence. . . . You feel peaceful and tranquil in this place. . . . Relax. . . . Here, all is well.

Use your extrasensory perception to take in all that's around. . . . In the silence, you may be able to sense the presence of your playwright. Although your playwright is pure essence and is beyond form and substance, it can appear to you in many different ways.

Keep silent and wait. Perhaps you'll see an ethereal form that looks a lot like you. . . . You may hear a rustle of movement . . . or feel a gentle touch. Allow the scene to unfold naturally.

This is the realm of Truth. Surrender into it. . . . Your playwright-Self is beyond thought and is wise beyond understanding. Open your mind to this immense knowing. . . . Be your infinite mind!

Your playwright-Self loves you more deeply than you can feel with all your emotions. Open your heart to unconditional, inclusive love. . . . You are loved just as you are! . . . You belong! . . . Rest in this love as long as you like.

Your playwright-Self is free and has powerful energy, like the sun. Allow the life force to flow freely through your body. . . . Feel your vitality. . . . Feel strength and courage rising from within. . . . Feel the power of pure being!

You and your playwright are two dimensions of one reality. Although your physical self has particular human characteristics, you are never separate from your nonphysical Self. You are distinct but not separate!

For a moment, experience yourSelf as the playwright. . . . As the playwright, from this high-frequency realm, be aware of your human cast of characters playing on the Earth stage. . . . Feel your love and appreciation for them. They are all reflecting different aspects of You. They are all your creations. They are playing out themes you have set into motion. They are doing the best they can in a world that is pulling them in many directions.

From here, what insights do you have into their present situation? . . . Are there any suggestions you can offer to help ease their plight? . . . In what way can you let them know how much you love them?

Is there a way to let them know that the universe is a safe place and that they have nothing to fear? . . . What message would you like to send back with the director?

Now, as your human directing-self, be aware that you can return any time to this dimension. It's only a thought away. The door is always open. This realm is ever-present within you.

The Self lives in eternity.
ROBERTO ASSAGIOLI

Step onto the marble disk again and activate the transport beam with your thought. Begin to float down the vortex of light . . . down . . . down . . . like a feather . . . until you land gently with both feet on the circle in the mysterium.

As the beam disperses, feel the weight of your imaginary body on the disk. Now step off and walk to the stairs . . . go down the steps . . . walk back onto the stage . . . down the aisle . . . out through the door . . . and back into this room. . . . Feel the weight of your physical body on your chair . . . and stretch.

For if a man should dream of heaven and, waking, find within his hand a flower as a token that he had really been there, what then, what then?
THOMAS WOLFE

❦

Your human experience is temporary, but your essential Self is eternal. You are indestructible. Nothing can truly harm you. You need not dwell on the past nor worry about the future. Just enjoy today and allow your playwright to reveal your purpose from one moment to the next.

✍ *Like a dream, this experience may fade in memory. To keep it alive, make notes, even though you may find that putting it into words is difficult. Be aware that some experiences are best kept secret to preserve their energy. If you speak of this, share it only with those who honor your inner being.*

Enjoying
the
Play

Rehearsals

Developing character and gaining mastery of the forces that move you is what directing is all about! Think of it this way: You are the god of your inner universe and this is *your* play. You are the one responsible for evoking divine qualities in your lesser gods and for orchestrating their performance on Earth.

The whole entourage knows when you help an actor to become a star. When one shines, all are illuminated. All benefit. The flame you fan has the power to enlighten the whole inner world. And the outer world as well. Yes, you have the power to change the course of history. If you doubt this, imagine how the world would be different today if Adolf Hitler had helped his inner Child heal from the daily thrashings his father inflicted on him when he was young. Here was a man who destroyed millions of people in an attempt to silence the voice of his father, who kept appearing in his nightmares. Analyst Alice Miller studied Hitler's childhood and explained in her book, *For Your Own Good*, "Had he [Hitler] made the entire world his victim, he still would not have been able to banish his introjected father from his bedroom, for one's own unconscious cannot be destroyed by destroying the world."

One distraught actor on the World Stage can create hell for the rest of us. That's why we must do all that we can to heal the wounds of the past and make the changes within. We must heal from the inside out. Cleaning up our own act first is the most important gift we can give other players on the World Stage.

Now that you know the steps of directing, you can begin to work consciously with your actors to coordinate their activities and pull the play together. Directing the group involves experimentation and practice. To help with your rehearsals, here's a very brief summary of directing.

A VERY BRIEF SUMMARY OF DIRECTING
Recognize your actors.
Accept their heartfelt desires.
Empower their star qualities.

Life is not a rehearsal.
DAVID BRUDNOY

Through daydreams our brains put us through mental rehearsals and keep us aware of the unfinished business of our lives.
JEROME SINGER

A bad rehearsal . . . prevents an actor from conveying the thoughts of the playwright— his main job.
STANISLAVSKI

In moving forward, call the members of your cast to leave their old ways behind and follow you in a radical reorientation toward life. By working together and sharing secret fears, hopes, griefs, and desires, you build among yourselves a feeling of intimacy and partnership.

As you go about your day, observe patterns in your controversies. Actors are famous for polarizing issues. *It's the drama*! You may discover polarities on the physical level (Fat self vs. Thin self), the emotional level (Weepy Willow vs. Stiff Upper Lip), or the mental level (Simple Simon vs. Genie the Genius).

Conflicts might arise between the Pacifist and the General (love and will), Betty Crocker and Amelia Earhart (safety and adventure), Professor Higgins and Rambo (intelligence and will), Macho Mac and Delicate Rose (masculinity and femininity), Nebish and Mensch (loser and real man), the Handyman and the Couch Potato (activity and passivity), the Hermit and the Party Animal (introversion and extroversion), the Lover and the Writer (heart and mind), or Mother Mary and the Whore (sacred and profane).

In the first act of the play, you recognize which actors are in conflict and what the theme is about. Then, often in the second act, the antagonism is full-blown and you can't imagine how it could ever work out. This is the place where you're tempted to get up and leave. But even if you don't like the performance and you do try to leave, it doesn't work. Your actors come after you, because they have a deep hunger for resolution. That's why you need all three acts. You need to stay and create the solution in the final scene. Without being too dramatic, I could say, *if you don't resolve, you can't evolve.*

However, don't blame yourself for pain or mistakes. When you experience suffering (and you will), simply *stop*. Take off the mask you're wearing and step back. Ask what story you are telling yourself. (Remember, *it's just a story.*) Which *part* of you is suffering? What does it want?

Over time, you'll develop more confidence in orchestrating the show. Your actors will become more cooperative, and you'll be surprised how rewarding it is to work together *consciously.*

The contribution of the Fool to our lives is resilience, the capacity to get up and try again.
CAROL PEARSON

Mistakes are part of the dues one pays for a full life.
SOPHIA LOREN

A Script: Cotton Mather and Dionysus

The following story demonstrates the value and effectiveness of conscious directing.

In an Inner Theatre workshop, as part of the program, participants attended an "Actors' Party," in which they made masks and dressed as one of their actors. Greg, a lawyer in his mid-fifties, came dressed as Cotton Mather (a New England Puritan minister). In playing Cotton, Greg became aware of another actor who was upset because he (the other actor) was not getting equal attention. Greg called this other part "Dionysus," after the Greek god who escaped regular routine to experience ecstasy.

Vaguely aware that the war between Cotton and Dionysus had been going on for years, Greg called the two together to see what their fight was about. Sitting in his director's chair, he placed both in front of him. He then stepped into each position, enacted their conflict, and allowed their story to unfold. This is the script, as Greg recaptured it in his journal.

The Exalted Apogee

DIRECTOR: Okay, I'd like to hear from the two of you. What's the problem?

COTTON: We don't have a lot of time. I'll just get right to it. [to Dionysus] You are irresponsible! You can't be counted on. You would just as soon play as think. The world was not made by playing. Thinking is key! Thinking is what gave us progress. Thinking is how you avoid the dangers of life, and let me tell you, there are dangers aplenty.

Let me show you. I have brought some books with all of the great thinking of the ages. Toynbee on history (eleven volumes), T. S. Eliot, Healing and Medicine, Myths, Dreams and Religion, the Rise and Fall of the Great Powers . . . I could go on and on, but you wouldn't pay any attention. You are too busy dreaming. You just put your little head back and point your horns to heaven and pretend to be blissful. [feeling disgust]

Even Jesus said you had to think. He told ten virgins to light their lamps. In advance! And be ready. He was no fool. He knew you had to use your mind. You had to be *with it* even then. Get ready for the worst and be damned glad if you get through. Few be they who really survive this earth.

But you come along and all you want to do is *swing*. That is cute. To the Greeks and the moderns, "swing" meant something. And it is not, nor ever was, responsible, or useful, or wise, whatever it means.

I am just trying to look out for you. You never would do it yourself.

DIONYSUS*:* Are you finished?

COTTON: Maybe. It depends on whether you answer responsibly.

DIONYSUS: There is a whole lot more to life than the mind. Talk about books! [points to his own pile of books to back up his argument] What about all the books on our shelves that you did not mention? We have here: *Anna Akhmatova*, the finest tragic Russian poetess of this century; and volumes of Russian art; and *Crime and Punishment*; and music tapes to fill a band box.

You didn't say anything about the moonlight on a clear night, or the wind in your hair and the wonderful way it feels—your cheek caressed by the breath from some Olympian spring. You didn't say anything about love, about joy, about the way it feels to be at the top of the swing.

You make fun of swingers, but what about the way it feels on the Greek vases, just at the apogee of the swing's arc, at the top, weightless, just before you come back down. We always knew, we Dionysians, that the moment does not last. Of course not. But if you don't push the swing to the height of the arc, you never know that instant of breathless freedom at the top, just before you come back down again. That is what we bring to the table. That is what you—in your somewhat crammed, stuffed, overweight head—forget.

More than forget it, you kill it. You are death to ecstasy, old man. You are the compromiser, a dealer with the future, like a card shark with destiny. You just want to play the odds. To you, intuition is superstition. But you know what? There are a lot of people these days who are writing books, yes books, about the importance of ecstasy and intuition!

And that, unhappily, is more than anyone can say for you. With all your mind and intellect, you have yet to finish a book. Why not? I don't know. Maybe if you could bring your heart into the act, tune into your body, you could finish something.

COTTON: Unkindest cut of them all! You not only have no responsibility, but you also have no mercy. That is the way it is with the free life. You get a man down, tease him about his failures, and then *whap!*, boot him in the teeth about the fact that he never finishes the books that he is writing.

Of course, we don't finish the things we start because, just when the hard part comes, when it is serious time, you come in and say to our man [the director], okay, time out, time for a breather, time for a Coke, time for a movie, time for a football game, time for a walk through the garden to check the carrots. Can you imagine how silly that is, walking through the garden, checking the last 1/16" growth of the carrots, carrots you checked only *this morning,* when there is writing, *serious* writing to do?

Can you imagine what the gods in heaven, your gods on Mt. Olympus even, must be saying when the little man with horns comes into the room and says to our author here, "Tired, child? Well, come on, let's get a little fresh air!" Give me a break! The Olympians, who probably don't exist anyway, are laughing their hedonistic hearts out, singing for joy over the collapse of another human effort that could have led this tortured Homo sapiens one small step forward in evolution.

That's all you get, you know. One small bit of time to contribute, one small step to try to ease the suffering and grief on this planet. This place is in a horrible mess. And you say, "Well, mess is part of the beauty of life."

Mess is pain, man, pure pain. Pain in Somalia. Pain in Bosnia. Pain here in River City.

But you and the Time-Out Team take tea in the morning, tea in the afternoon, tea after dinner, and tea in the intermission of the opera. Tea, tea, tea. As if the world survived on crumpets and strumpets!

DIONYSUS: You sound a little angry.

COTTON: I just don't feel like you ever really hear.

DIONYSUS: I don't much, that's true. It's hard to hear all that self-righteousness, and you rule out all the tools of my side. All you want to do is figure this thing out with the mind, and that is not what I have to offer. I respect the mind, but it is not everything.

COTTON: I suppose it is not *everything*.

DIRECTOR: [Taking my director's chair, I see that both are presenting their sides, but the discussion is going nowhere. I decide to steer the dialogue in a new direction.] How could you two begin to cooperate? What do you have to offer each other?

DIONYSUS: [to Cotton] I don't want to throw everything you say out the window. I know that you are worried. And you are right, of course, about the pain on the planet. I'm not trying to deny that. I'm just trying to find a more complete response to it.

COTTON: It is dangerous when you give in to the body. I'm concerned that you could seduce women, political constituencies, editors, and half the civilized world if you use your "charm thing."

DIONYSUS: Actually, I think you are right. I could be seductive. Whatever we do on the road to ecstasy, we will have to be aware of the dangers. But maybe we should not give up the quest just because it is dangerous?

DIRECTOR: [Sitting back in the director's chair, I realize that the voices could have been those of my father in a conversation we never could have had. His is the voice of Cotton Mather; mine—that of the eternal youth. I decide to bring my father—who is no longer alive—into the scene and have a direct conversation with him.]

DIONYSUS AS THE SON: [In this chair, I sit for some minutes before I can speak. I take in the prospect of talking like this to the man I admired most in all the world.]

I never loved anyone as much as you. [I begin to cry uncontrollably.] You were the most wonderful, the wisest and kindest man that ever I knew. You were fair, and you tried as hard as a person could try. [A long pause, trying to control my emotion.]

But you weren't all that you could have been. You came to the end of your life and there was something missing. You were loved by us all, but you didn't get something for yourself that you wanted. And you stuffed it. You learned to live without it. We all loved you because you never complained. But you also never got to the height of your ability to explore and enjoy, and you were tight inside.

All I want to do is go the next step, to get past the tight inside.

COTTON AS THE FATHER: [Deeply touched.] You are right. Right about me. And right to go the next step.

DIONYSUS AS THE SON: [Regaining control, tears drying up.] It is not that I want to forget my head, or forget the intellectual life. It's just that I get sick a lot now, and there is some reason, and it may be that I took the message of hard work so literally that my physical system is breaking down somehow.

I have to go beyond the slogans. It *is* dangerous. But now it is dangerous not to experience the ecstasy of life.

COTTON AS THE FATHER: Go for it, son. I want you to experience the fullness of life. I want you to do what I was unable to do. Do it for yourself and for your sons. I give you my permission and my blessing.

DIRECTOR: [I can tell he means it. I realize that something important is shifting inside of me, and I begin to envision what it would be like for Cotton and Dionysus to pool their perspectives and resources. It's important for me to do this for me and for my children, otherwise I will pass the conflict on to them.]

DIONYSUS: [to Cotton] You know what? I think we can work this thing out together.

COTTON: Yeah, I think so, too.

DIONYSUS: I feel relaxed. Like the tension is out of it. There are dangers in life at the height of the arc of the swing, but I feel like we can go for it and not fall out.

COTTON: I feel. . .

DIONYSUS: You *feel*! You mean you *feel*, like in *not thinking*?

COTTON: Yeah. I feel excited about what you have to offer me—like we can have ecstasy without getting drunk and going unconscious, and without seducing women and ruining our marriage. We'll have to talk more about how to do this thing together.

DIRECTOR: Don't forget, I'm here with you. You are both feeling vulnerable now, but it seems like *right now* we are experiencing the top of the swing—the ecstasy of being real.

Dark Comedy

*The local university
wants to grant Pain
tenure, but the students
insist his teaching is
overrated.*
J. RUTH GENDLER

Sometimes we suffer *too much*. In such times, the Divine Comedy turns dark and the pain is intense. In *Inevitable Grace*, Piero Ferrucci talks about the crippling effect pain can have on us. "When suffering becomes too strong, it imprisons our attention with its impersonal brutality, kills our enthusiasm, turns our hopes into empty dreams. Its incomprehensibility undermines the psychophysical structure we have come to know as ourselves. In pain, be it mental or physical, we are faced with the concrete possibility of our own annihilation."

We could die! We could be engulfed by our difficult situation. If, in our pain, we give up our dreams, our hopes, our faith; if we become bitter or hateful; if we betray our self or deny our soul—that is real tragedy! It's a tragedy because pain doesn't have to destroy us. As we teeter on the ragged edge of destruction, we can remember that we are more than our body, more than this situation. *We* will not be destroyed.

Furthermore, we are not alone in our suffering. During dark times we can find comfort in two ways. One way is to step back from the actor who is distressed or in pain, then take this suffering one in our arms and hold it close. As director, we can come into resonance with the depth of misery this part of us is feeling.

*Experience the pain.
Let us not fear its
impact on ourselves
or others. We will not
shatter, for we are not
objects that can break.*
JOANNA MACY

Another way is to remain in the pain, but to relax in the embrace of your playwright (or your angel, or Christ) and *together* go deeper into the fear, pain, or grief until you move through it to the other side. Yes, there is always another side, because pain is not permanent.

We can make it through the darkest of nights if we know we're not alone. We can go through hell if we know that the presence of the divine is leading us through. Once, when I experienced great emotional pain after the breakup of a relationship, I wanted the whole universe to understand my feelings of agony. So without using my physical voice, I screamed inside so loud that the farthest galaxies got my message. (In the inner world, making a noise that terrible is possible!) After I shook the whole universe with my cry, I felt a wonderful relief. At that moment, I realized how important it is for our pain-racked cries to be heard and understood.

Yes, we can walk with our inner cast and with each other through times of suffering and loss. We can be carried on the wings of divine love. And when we make it through, we'll know the meaning of triumph over tragedy.

Illusion of Death

The phone rings. My sister-in-law in Kansas informs me that my beloved mom just had a heart attack and is unconscious in the Intensive Care Unit in Hutchinson. Totally unprepared for this, I tearfully scramble to pack some things then drive ten endless hours through the night to be at her bedside.

Not knowing what to expect, I enter the room and gently hold her hand—the hand that has been here for me all my life. Arousing from unconsciousness, she opens her eyes and squeezes my hand in response. Unable to talk with the tubes in her nose and mouth, she looks deep into my eyes, smiles, nods her characteristic nod, and closes her eyes for the last time. Trying to be strong for her, I whisper that if this is her time to go, it's okay, because our love for each other is eternal and our souls will live on together.

The family gathers in the room. I caress Mom's hair and face and kiss her forehead. My youngest brother notices that each time I kiss her, the EEG registers a blip as the line decreases, then becomes straight. Silently and gracefully, she slips out of her human costume and leaves her body behind with us.

As I stand by her in grief, I recall a dream I had two years earlier. In the dream, Mom is talking to me as we sort through old clothing. On a table lies a piece of cloth that looks like her body. She says, "Fold it up and put it in the Goodwill box." I follow her instructions and we continue to sort.

Now, holding her lifeless hand, I'm aware of how attached I am to her physical body. I don't want to lay her costume in the Goodwill box. She's only seventy-three and I had planned to have her in my play for another twenty years. She was such an important, loving player in my life. I wonder how I can possibly live without my mother.

In subsequent days, my daughter-self grieves deeply, missing Momma and feeling the wrenching pain of separation. On another level, my director-self feels love and compassion for the daughter, and

When in the end, we render up our masks to earth and sky and sea, in God we shall discern who did and said the better thing.
TOMMASO CAMPANELLA

is with her in her agony. On yet another level, my playwright-Self is deeply connected to Mom's spirit and knows *she* is not dead. Mom says to me, "It's only my body that isn't with you anymore. I'm still here." Our souls laugh at the outrageous illusion that *she* could ever die.

Death feels like a tragedy to those who forget that they are the soul playing a masquerade. I guess for them, it *is* a tragedy. But for those who remember who they are, death is the grand finale on the Earth stage, not the finale of the soul's Play.

Part of the Divine Comedy is the pain of endings. And while pain and grief are deeply significant experiences, they are transient emotions. They come and they go. What is ultimately reliable is the soul behind all the masks of emotion and human experience. The soul remains ever stable, steadfast, and radiant!

✍ Identify the times and ways you have suffered throughout your life and write them down. Has pain weakened you or made you stronger? How has each experience influenced your life?

The great tragedy of life is not that men perish, but that they cease to love.
W. SOMERSET MAUGHAM

The Empty Stage

In the seasons of life, sometimes the curtain is down and the stage seems empty. Sometimes the performance falls apart and the unknown seems unbearable. In these dark times, you don't know which way to turn, or what to do.

This "coming apart" may be experienced as a nervous breakdown, a midlife crisis, or as any number of other difficulties. It may come as the result of a job loss, a bankruptcy, the breakup of a significant relationship, the death of a loved one, an illness, a depression, or a loss of faith. In each case, you are required to make a major change. The old way of doing things no longer works.

During times of disorientation, you may feel the agony of your limitations. You may be impatient with yourself for not being more clever or resilient. You may forget that there is a higher order in chaos.

The empty stage represents a time of transition, a time to change scenes and props. By their very nature, transitions are temporary; they do not last forever. The end of an old show is not the end of your life. There will be another program—another beginning and another ending. This is the time to create the space for that new beginning.

Still, waiting on the empty stage is difficult, as people who've been there can testify. Ellie, a massage therapist going through a personal identity crisis, explained that she was feeling extremely vulnerable and unprotected, as though she had "no skin." Sharon, a young physician, whose marriage was crumbling, described her feeling as one of "being in a void"—a nowhere place with nowhere to go. She was not sure she was strong enough to make it on her own. And Marion, a computer programmer, questioned whether he was "going crazy" as he let go of his profession in search of another. He reported that he felt like a foreigner in places that had previously been familiar.

During these times of change, when the old way doesn't work and the new way is not yet revealed, you may find comfort in knowing that *this too shall pass*. You may also find the following suggestions helpful in reaffirming your deeper knowing, love, and will.

Sometimes I wake up Grumpy; other times I let him sleep.
BUMPER STICKER

Destructuring is the undoing, the coming apart . . . of some of our natural ways of seeing, of knowing ourselves, of relating to the world.
ANNE YEOMANS

To drop into the void of the unknown is an act of courage. To wait patiently there is an act of faith.
GWEN HARRISON

*The tragic events and
the glorious epiphanies
in our lives offer
opportunities for us
to learn most
accurately who we are
and how to nurture
our soul.*
MICHAEL MEADE

*In the great crises of
life, when existence
itself is threatened,
the soul attains
transcendent powers.*
STRINDBERG

What to do when the stage is empty

AWARENESS: Trust that there *is* a purpose in what is happening, even in the midst of your unknowing. Be open to recognize new opportunities when they come.

Affirm: *I trust myself to know in time.*

LOVE: Feel all your feelings, especially your exquisite vulnerability. Be gentle and find ways to nurture yourself each day.

Affirm: *I always have my Self. I am not alone.*

WILL: Take responsibility for your responses to the situation. Although you have little control over your environment, circumstances, and other people, you do have control over your own actions.

Affirm: *I have the power to choose my responses.*

I appreciate Julia Cameron's way of handling tough times. She writes in *The Artist's Way*, "In times of pain, when the future is too terrifying to contemplate and the past too painful to remember, I have learned to pay attention to right now. . . . In the exact now, we are all, always, all right."

If you focus on what you can gain (the objective) rather than what you might lose or are losing or have lost (the problem), you may more easily recognize the special meaning and purpose of your situation. In any case, you are never alone. Like young Luke Skywalker in *Star Wars*, you can tune in to The Force. Luke listened to the wisdom of Obi Wan Kenobi who said, "The Force is an energy field created by all living things. It surrounds us, it penetrates us, it binds galaxies together." Certainly if this is true (and I believe it is), we can trust what is unfolding day by day!

Peak Performances

Now and then you experience times when you are simply and fully yourself—present to life as it is. Instead of practicing, or rehearsing to get better, you are mindfully aware of *now*. When past, present, and future converge, we live the *holy instant*.

Such golden moments may be momentous or quietly ordinary. They may come when you're receiving a special award, when you're involved in a creative project, or when you're watching the last crimson rays of the sunset. You may experience them when you're embracing someone you love, when you're listening to the birds in your back yard, or when you're playing a musical instrument by yourself. You may recognize the holy instant when you're dancing, preparing dinner, or resting in bed with an illness.

What's happening may be beautiful or painful. It doesn't matter. What is, *is*. In these moments, you're not experiencing the separation of your body, mind, and spirit. You're not trying to avoid pain or grasp pleasure. Instead of struggling in a *drama,* you simply are the *play*!

As director, one of your goals is to create the conditions in which you can experience more moments of this mindful awareness. Of course, as you know full well, there is a time to learn new parts and to sweat through rehearsals, but there is also a time to relax and simply be. This is the dance between *becoming* and *being*.

As humans, our goal is not to become perfect (an impossible feat), but to live each moment as consciously as possible. Even when our cast is struggling, we can capture moments when we experience what T. S. Eliot described as the "still point of the turning world."

That still point is the space between thoughts, the pause between breaths, the instant at the top of the swing that Dionysus described to Cotton Mather in the script we examined earlier. In this moment, we enter a *unified field* where we discover that everything is connected and has purpose and meaning.

To live the holy moment, we must trust the flow of life and take one step at a time, without forcing our act. In fact, we perform at our peak when we . . .

There is no "performance." There is just this moment.
JON KABAT-ZINN

The heroic hours of life do not announce their presence by drum and trumpet.
BENJAMIN CARDOZO

We need to live our lives with a keen awareness of each moment, but against the backdrop of eternity.
ROBERTO ASSAGIOLI

. . . are present in the moment;

. . . feel connected to life and nature;

. . . trust and accept the full range of our emotions;

. . . are awake, intuitive, and open to new ideas;

. . . are innovative and creative;

. . . care about others and the success of the larger Play;

. . . trust that the Play is unfolding for the good of all.

Violinist Nadja Salerno-Sonnenberg, winner of the prestigious Naumburg Awards, knows what it's like to give a peak performance. "She is the music," says conductor Michael Tilson Thomas. In a *Christian Science Monitor* interview, Nadja describes her experience like this: "I feel possessed when I play. Possessed, meaning that everything is one, the orchestra I'm playing with, the piece I'm playing, the conductor I'm working with, the violin under my chin, and the sounds that are coming out. Everything is just one. I call it playing in the zone. What a feeling! It makes you feel like everything you've ever done in your whole life is worth it."

Those who have watched Isadora Duncan dance say that she becomes her soul, dancing. Magic happens when people perform at their peak and the audience shares in their joy. For example, this is how Duncan's sister-in-law described the audience's response during one of her performances: "When she danced the *Blue Danube*, her simple waltzing forward and back, like the oncoming and receding waves on the shore, had such an ecstasy of rhythm that audiences became frenzied with the contagion of it, and could not contain themselves, but rose from their seats, cheering, applauding, laughing and crying. . . . We felt as if we had received the blessing of God."

At this kind of zenith, one not only has a feeling of blessing and oneness, but also a realization that there is an order to life. Astronaut Edgar Mitchell was overcome with emotion when he saw the whole of Earth from space. He has written: "It began with the breathtaking experience of seeing planet Earth floating in the immensity of space—the incredible beauty of a splendid blue-and-white jewel floating in the vast black sky. I underwent a religious-like peak experience, in which the presence of divinity became almost palpable, and I *knew* that life in the universe was not just an accident based on random processes."

The public for which masterpieces are intended is not on this earth.
THORNTON WILDER

No, the universe is not based on random processes. There is a purpose to every element of the Play.

Curtains rise and curtains fall. When we have successfully completed one scene, we discover another twist in the plot to resolve—another aspect of destiny to fulfill. Life isn't about drifting on the glory of our past achievements! Our playwright doesn't allow us to become bored with the known, but rather gives us opportunities to play ever more festive and rewarding parts.

In truth, life is an awesome *ongoing saga*.

✍ What peak experiences, revelations, insights, and awakenings have you experienced? Write these down and note how each has influenced your life.

I believe in a festive God.
JULIA CAMERON

Celebrating Life

Celebrate the privilege of living today and enjoy the following Ode to Life!

To Life! It is a beautiful day in your inner world and you are in a lush, magnificent meadow. The sky is blue, the air is fresh, the birds are singing, the flowers are blooming, and the animals are forming a circle for the celebration that is about to take place. Greet the new day with gratitude.

Today you'll bring your cast of characters to the circle to celebrate life and all that's present for you.

Feel the energy of a newborn baby in your heart. Feel your vulnerability, your purity, and your innocence. You have just been born into an exciting new life. Now is the time to celebrate your newness.

Feel the energy of the child in your heart. Feel your eagerness to explore, to be touched and held, to play and run and gather flowers. Feel your delight in the animals, your fearlessness, and your awe at all the things around you. Follow the bugs, chew on blades of grass, wade

Greet the morning with the radiant joy of gratitude . . .
MARY BAKER EDDY

in a stream, roll down a little hill. Celebrate your wonder and happiness, and your openness to life.

Feel the energy of an adolescent in your heart. Feel your curiosity and enthusiasm for life. There are so many things you want to do, so many lives you want to live. Feel your optimism and eagerness to become the great person you know you are. Feel your growing need to be independent, but also your need to depend on others. Celebrate your belief in what life has to offer.

Feel the energy of nurturing parents in your heart—the inner mother and father, who have a deep capacity to love and forgive. Celebrate your ability to nurture life.

Feel your desire to make a living for yourself and the ones you love in a way that nourishes your spirit. There are things you want to create, talents you want to express, gifts you want to give. Celebrate your commitment to play at your work.

In this meadow, feel the synergy of all your players. Today be willing to seek the highest truth, accept yourself as you are, and act with integrity. Today, take one step at a time, breathe deeply, and enjoy the holy moment. This is the Play that life is meant to be.

The world is only for celebration. Manifestation is just a Cosmic Drama to be enjoyed.
SRI H. W. L. POONJA

Plays and More Plays

At the same time you are the director of your inner theatre, you are also an actor on FAMILY, COMMUNITY, and ORGANIZATIONAL stages. We are all actors in many shows.

In the outer theatre, we are often cast in roles we don't want, but we dutifully play them rather than to cause a disturbance. For example, in the family, you may play the role of Black Sheep, Rebel, Rescuer, Peacemaker, or Baby. Some babies in the family are never allowed to grow up, and some oldest children are never allowed to be children. Recently I had a conversation with a friend (an only child in the family) who has played the role of Parent to her mother ever since she can remember. Even on my friend's wedding day, her mother acted like a child—refusing to do this, insisting on doing that—demanding special attention the whole time instead of making things easier for her daughter.

Or take the community drama. Here you may be known as the Expert Investor, the Town's Preoccupied Grandmother, the Wily Opportunist, the Greatest Volunteer, or the Pain-in-the-Neck-Activist.

On the work stage, you might be cast in the role of The Big Honcho, the Slave Driver, the Fast-Track Manager, El Groucho, the Showcase Minority person, the Flirt, or the Sassy Secretary.

Often we play the roles we are given until we realize that our voice is important and that we can change the script. Eventually we discover that the more authentic we are and the more we live by our own lights, the easier it is to evoke the star qualities in those around us.

Now you may take what you have learned as an inner theatre director and apply it to plays that involve other people.

We must serve the play by serving each other.
UTA HAGEN

The Family Play

✍ *In considering your family, you may choose to focus on your extended family of origin, your immediate family, or the family with which you have most in common. Write the answers to these questions on a sheet of paper.*

Which roles do you play in the family?

What drama (issue, problem) is presently in the spotlight on your family stage?

Where does the present scene take place?

Who are the main actors on the stage? Where are you on the stage?

On paper, sketch a typical scene as it is now.

What is missing?

Does intelligence, love, or will need the most development? Explain.

What could be the name of this drama?

Sketch another version of this scene the way you would like it to be.

What would you be willing to do to make this new scene a reality?

The Community Play

Self-actualizing people are . . . involved in a cause outside their own skin.
ABRAHAM MASLOW

✍ *In considering your community, would you describe it as a large city, small town, intimate neighborhood, or rural community? You can answer the following questions by focusing on your larger community or on your particular special interest group (church, school, women's club, athletic association, ecological society, other).*

From your perspective, what central drama (issue, problem) is currently in the spotlight?

Who are the main actors on the stage? Where are you on the stage?

On paper, sketch a typical scene as it is now.

What is missing?

Does intelligence, love, or will need the most development? Explain.

What could be the name of this drama?

Sketch another version of this scene the way you would like it to be.

What would you be willing to do to make this new scene a reality?

The Occupational Play

✍ *Now that you know how to be an inner theatre director, you can become a successful director or manager in the outer world as well. In this exercise, notice how the three steps of directing can be applied to the Organizational Play.*

First Step: Recognition

As you consider your work situation, what drama (issue, problem) is in the spotlight?

Where does the scene take place?

Who are the main actors on the stage?

Where are you on the stage?

Does intelligence, love, or will need the most development? Explain.

What could be the name of the present play?

Sketch a typical scene on paper.

Second Step: Acceptance

What are your predominant feelings in this situation?

What is missing?

What do you want for yourself?

What do you want for your organization?

What do you want even more? (What essential quality can become the shining feature in the business?)

What is it like to know you already have this within yourself? What is it like to know that this quality is already present (albeit dormant) in the business?

You can't manage others until you manage yourself.
JOHN CULLEN

. . . the man who is detached from results and tries only to do his best without thought of profit or power or prestige does not waver when difficulties come.
EKNATH EASWARAN

Third Step: Empowerment

As an actor in this play, what are you not willing to do at work? (your "no")

What are you willing to do instead? (your "yes")

What would you need in order to play your part most effectively? (funds, equipment, support, time)

How would this benefit your organization? . . . your community?

How could your organization benefit the larger Play of humanity?

What new script is possible? What could be the name of the new play?

What is one thing you are willing to do to enhance your work performance.

World-Class Actors

At the same time we are directors of our inner theatre, we are also actors on the World Stage. We are all part of the Universal Play. The word *uni-verse* means *one-song*. We are notes of the same song— actors in the same mysterious, ever-unfolding Production.

We must balance the attention we give to our inner world with the attention we give to this outer world. In his book *Earth in the Balance,* Al Gore encourages people to find the balance between "individual concerns and commitment to the community" and between "love for the natural world and love for our wondrous civilization." A good actor not only develops its character, but also takes responsibility for the success of the whole show. How an actor relates to other actors in a play will determine the quality of a performance.

The state is the individual writ large.
PLATO

What is now taking place on the Global Stage is largely a collective reflection of what is occurring within each person. Most players are perplexed about who they are and their relationship to the larger show. People struggle to do the best they can, but many lack the inner strength to adapt. The result is emotional numbing, illness, addiction, poverty, consumerism, criminal activity, and a disregard for the environment. For most people, visions for a better life are obscure.

. . . the global crisis facing our planet is the sum total of the billions of daily actions of individuals, industries, and governments.
MOSTAFA TOLBA
EARTH SUMMIT, 1992

Behind all the stiff upper lips and masks of bravado, we are grieving inside. We are grieving our lost innocence, our feelings of alienation, our timidity in standing up for what is right, and our failure to imagine new ways of being. We're grieving our lost childhood and adolescence. We're grieving because we've misunderstood who we are and have disempowered ourselves.

Sick and tired of suffering, we want more. We want to feel innocent again. We want to belong. We want to stand up for what is right and to imagine new ways of being! Fortunately, the World Play isn't over yet. Since all the men and women are the actors, we still have an opportunity to change the show.

Confusion doesn't need to be our primary mental state, helplessness doesn't need to be our basic feeling, and tragedy doesn't need to be our overriding theme. As world actors, we understand that there are alternatives to watching our Home Theater self-destruct.

You cannot hope to build a better world without improving the individuals. . . . each of us must work for his own improvement, and at the same time . . . aid those to whom we think we can be most useful.
MARIE CURIE

In the past, we thought we could let others make decisions for us. We thought we could let politicians, bureaucrats, bankers, and priests call the shots. That time is over. We can no longer let others do our thinking. *It's imperative that we, as individuals, think, feel, and act from our own center of integrity—our center of intelligence, love, and will.*

Carl Jung declared: "If things go wrong in the world, this is because . . . something is wrong with me. Therefore, if I am sensible, I shall put myself right first." Sharing a similar view, Mikhail Gorbachev, former General Secretary of the Soviet Union, addressed readers of the world in his book *Perestroika: New Thinking for Our Country and the World.* He passionately emphasized the fact that the *initial* task of restructuring (or Perestroika) is "to ensure that everyone feels as if he or she is the master of the country, of his enterprise, office, or institute. This is the main thing."

While most of us are not heads of state in the outer world, all of us are heads of state in our inner world. We are responsible for creating internal order, which in turn influences social order. Yes, the more skillfully we play our particular parts, the more we'll bring out the star-qualities in others and make the world a better place to be—or a *better Play to see.*

A New World Play

Each of us can join the ranks of the visionaries and pathfinders who are pulled forward by the future. Together we can find innovative solutions to today's problems and create new scripts. We can define new ways of living on Earth. With help from modern technological developments like the Internet, we can exchange creative ideas, insights, and information with others from around the world.

Considering humanity's rich internal and external resources, imagine what is possible for our new World Play to become. To start the flow of your thinking, imagine the Global Play in which . . .

Individuals learn to take charge of their inner cast of characters and develop their potential.

Children are conceived in love and are nurtured by parents who help them develop their intelligence, love, and will.

Couples and families commit to supporting each other in developing their many star-qualities.

Education is integrated into all aspects of life and is designed to bring all members of society to their highest level of functioning.

Information flows freely throughout the world and knowledge is shared to generate new theories, inventions, and technologies.

Psychology encompasses and addresses the full spectrum of growth and development of the inner self (pre-birth to transcendence) and develops effective methods of diagnosis and healing at each stage.

Health-care professions develop the field of medical synthesis and holistic medicine, bringing a spiritual perspective to support the natural process of healing.

Religious denominations and spiritual seekers recognize the fundamental unity that underlies all religion.

Prayer for guidance in discovering the Universal Playwright's vision for our planet becomes a common activity.

Business organizations encourage employees to develop imagination and creativity to increase job satisfaction and productivity.

Political emphasis is placed on ecological awareness and social responsibility.

Man is now the managing director of evolution in the universe.
SIR JULIAN HUXLEY

We need to use the suffering of the twentieth century as compost, so that together we can create flowers for the twenty-first century.
THICH NHAT HANH

Political groups transcend adversarial positions to create a higher synthesis in national and world politics.

Women are fairly represented in positions of leadership, using intuition, magic, and art, to invent new ways of living safely on Earth.

An operational peace outlaws all weapons of mass murder and creates effective methods for nonviolent conflict resolution.

Financiers consider long-term goals (including ecological concerns) in directing the economy, as opposed to short-term profits.

Commodities, resources, and services flow freely, and structures continue to be created for the distribution of wealth in the world.

The areas of wilderness, wildlife, pristine watershed, and forest are preserved, so all people can enjoy natural land and wildlife.

The environment is protected, conserved, blessed, and honored as sacred; people give back to Earth as much as they take.

There is hope if people will begin to awaken that spiritual part of themselves—that heartfelt acknowledgment that we are the caretakers of this planet!
BROOKE MEDICINE EAGLE

An Important Player

Throughout his life, Buckminster Fuller, a discoverer and inventor, kept asking himself the following question: *What is it on this planet that needs doing that I know something about, that probably won't happen unless I take responsibility for it?*

When you realize that you are an actor on the World Stage, you begin to understand that only you can play your part. No one else can take your place. You have something to give to others that no one else can provide. As Mahatma Gandhi observed, "Almost anything you do will seem insignificant but it is important that you do it. . . . You must be the change you wish to see in the world."

What do *you* contribute to the World Play?

As human actors, what we contribute is only limited by our imagination and our willingness to participate in creating the future. By enlisting the help of our playwright and powerful members of the supporting cast, we can enjoy co-creating solutions to difficult problems.

We can envision and enact **The Greatest Show on Earth!**

And that's the way it is.
WALTER CRONKITE

Appendix

An Innertaining Love Story

HOW INNER THEATRE WAS BORN

It happened one dark and stormy night, inside a cabin tucked securely away in the Sangre de Cristo Mountains. The times were unpredictable and turbulent, but for the lovers by the fireplace, the time was *high-time*. In a sensual embrace, the two passionately conceived something extraordinary. Their union was undoubtedly inspired by the gods and goddesses themselves.

But that takes place in Act II. To see what the play's all about, let's start at the beginning.

The time is the mid-twentieth century; the place, Florence, Italy. The spotlight shines on the rising, female star—Psychosynthesis. Her father is Roberto Assagioli, a gentle physician specializing in neurology and psychiatry.

Raised in this culturally rich city surrounded by the painting, sculpture, and architecture of the Middle Ages and the Renaissance, golden-haired Psychosynthesis develops a natural appreciation for music, art, nature, and religion. She spends considerable time with her older cousin, Psychoanalysis, son of Sigmund Freud, and with her Swiss friend, Carl Jung. All three friends are fascinated with the human psyche. Psycho*analysis* is primarily interested in exploring the nooks and crannies in the basement of the mind, while Psycho*synthesis* and Jung like searching for treasures in the upper rooms of the mysterium.

As the scene unfolds, you observe the adult Psychosynthesis working with people in ways that fire their imagination and renew their hope. She inspires them to be honest and real, and helps them develop the courage to follow their dreams. As she quietly goes about her work of healing, teaching, and guiding, she displays a fine intellect, a caring heart, and a gentle will.

Because of her universal perspective and great love for humanity, Psychosynthesis is keenly aware of the suffering experienced by so many in the world. She does her best to relieve pain and to help people develop a strong sense of self, but she recognizes her limitations. The first scene closes with Psychosynthesis sitting in her living room at the end of a full day, deeply concerned about the state of the world. The task of personal, social, and spiritual synthesis is great; her influence is small.

The second scene opens with all the flair of Hollywood, Broadway, and Silicon Valley combined. Alternating images and synchronized music pulsate irreverently, creating an effective backdrop for the drama of the male star—The Entertainer. With flair and panache, he steps into the spotlight and commands the attention of all those watching.

He is dashing, flamboyant, and charming, distinctly giving the impression that he's a man of the world. Skillfully, he uses many aspects of the media to portray the colorful pageant of people's lives. Everyone seems to love him as he opens windows to the larger world of experience and introduces them to characters, human and mythical, of every type.

The Entertainer has a vivid imagination and a fine sense of humor, making him a constant source of *appealing surprise*. Yet, as engaging and magnificent as he is, he also has a dark side—a side he doesn't necessarily try to hide. He has a strong inclination to stimulate people's unresolved emotions and arouse their worst fears. He knows that terrifying, violent, and sexually explicit Horror Shows attract people who live on the ragged edge of destruction. Nevertheless, he finds it amusing—and profitable—to produce sensational dramas.

Having become very wealthy by being spectacular, The Entertainer sits in the lap of Luxury and hobnobs with the Rich and Famous. Outwardly he presents himself as "having it all," but inwardly he experiences a painful moral and spiritual emptiness. Sometimes when he's all alone, he asks himself: "Is this *it*?"

As the curtain opens on Scene III, you find The Entertainer strolling in a city park on a summer day. Birds peck at crumbs on the sidewalk and a squirrel darts from behind a tree. Except for an old man sleeping on the grass and a light-haired woman sitting under a tree in the distance, there is little human activity. As he walks along, The Entertainer mumbles to himself: "I have wealth. I have influence. So why do I feel so empty? What's missing?"

Nearby, Psychosynthesis sits under a tree on a quilt her parents made for her. She thinks of the people she loves and serves and a wave of sadness comes over her. Tears roll down her cheeks as The Entertainer strolls by.

He glances at her and pauses. The radiance behind her sorrow touches something deep inside. He takes out his handkerchief, leans over, and gently wipes her tears. She touches his hand and looks deeply into his eyes.

She sees, behind layers of blue charisma, his soul. "What is your name?" she asks softly.

"They call me The Entertainer, but I'm not sure anymore who I really am," he replies.

Studying him carefully, she says: "*You* are a great magician."

"You see that in me?" he asks in surprise.

"Yes," she nods. "You are a magician, but I think you have fooled even yourself. Am I right?"

"I think you may be," he confesses as he kneels beside her on the grass.

Leaning forward, Psychosynthesis reflects, "An Italian philosopher, Tommaso Campanella, once said, *In the theatre of the world, our souls play a masquerade, hiding themselves behind their bodies and their effects.* Perhaps you have forgotten that you are the soul playing a masquerade."

Listening intently, The Entertainer nods slightly and responds, "I feel successful professionally, but something definitely is missing. My performance lacks spirit. I make a lot of money, but on a deeper level, I'm really quite bored."

Smiling in understanding, Psychosynthesis continues, "When you remember who you are behind all your masks, your performance will take on a whole new meaning and purpose. Instead of meeting people on *one* dimension, you'll meet on *many.* You can give your audience opportunities to discover deeper truths of who they are. I believe this is how *real* magic happens."

Drawn to her insight and transparency, The Entertainer responds thoughtfully: "What you are saying makes sense. I need to think about it more. . . . But tell me, who are you?"

"My name is Psychosynthesis."

"Do they call you *Psycho* or *Syn* for short?" he asks teasingly.

"All that and more," she laughs. "It's amazing what people can do with a name."

"Tell me, dear woman. Why have you been crying? Why the tears?"

"I feel sad for all the people who struggle so hard," she explains in a subdued voice. "Most people are completely mesmerized by their daily dramas. My purpose is to *unmask the human spirit*—to help people really enjoy the play, but I feel limited in my ability to reach large groups of people. I feel sad about my limitations."

Trying hard to understand, The Entertainer responds: "I'm sure your sadness is legitimate, but come. *This is too important to take seriously.*"

Extending his hand, The Entertainer helps Psychosynthesis rise to her feet. Gaining her balance, she runs her fingers through her hair and manages a smile.

With a valiant bow, The Entertainer declares: "It would please me if you would join me for dinner, where we can continue our conversation."

Smiling, Psychosynthesis curtsies and whispers: "And it would delight me to accept!"

That's how it all started. In Act II, Scene I, we find the two spending more and more time together. Before long, Psychosynthesis is singing and dancing, and The Entertainer is preparing a script for a new, twenty-first century Divine Comedy.

In Scene II, the curtain opens to a loud clap of thunder. It is a dark and stormy night in the mountains. Inside a cozy cabin, before a flaming fireplace, Psychosynthesis and The Entertainer passionately embrace. Fully in love, they consciously conceive something new from heaven.

Outside, the storm quiets down, and only a soft rain can be heard on the windowpanes as the scene fades.

The last scene takes place months later. The couple, filled with excitement and joy, gives birth to their new creation, whom they call "Inner Theatre," or "IT" for short.

"IT's all in a name," the mother and father explain, laughing.

Inheriting the best from both parents, Inner Theatre naturally becomes dynamic and *innertaining*. Both innocent and worldly, IT denies nothing in the Play of Life and reminds people, in a fun way, who they have always been behind their costumes and masks.

Being magical, Inner Theatre can be found on the corner of Imagination Street and Adventure Avenue—inside your mind.

The curtain to Act III is now rising.

References

Aïvanhov, Omraam Mikhaël. *Daily Meditation.* Prosveta S. A., 1996.

Alighieri, Dante. *The Divine Comedy.* Random House, 1986.

Andrews, Robert, ed. *The Columbia Dictionary of Quotations.* New York: Columbia University Press, 1993.

Assagioli, Roberto. *Psychosynthesis: A Manual of Principles and Techniques.* New York: Penguin Books, 1976.

———. *The Act of Will.* New York: Viking, 1973.

———. *Transpersonal Development.* London: Crucible, 1991.

———. *Life as a Game and Stage Performance.* Monograph, 1983.

Boleslavsky, Richard. *Acting: The First Six Lessons.* New York: Theater Arts Books, 1933.

Breathnach, Sarah Ban. *Simple Abundance.* New York: Warner Books, 1995.

Cameron, Julia and Mark Bryan. *The Artist's Way.* Los Angeles: Jeremy Tarcher, 1992.

Cameron, Julia. *The Vein of Gold.* Los Angeles, Jeremy Tarcher, 1996.

Canfield, Jack and Mark Victor Hansen. *Chicken Soup for the Soul.* Florida: Health Communications, 1995.

Carlyon, Richard. *A Guide to the Gods.* New York: Quill, William Morrow, 1981.

Chödrön, Pema. *Wisdom of No Escape.* New York: Random House, 1991.

Chopra, Deepak. *Creating Affluence.* San Rafael, CA: New World Library, 1993.

———. *Seven Spiritual Laws of Success.* San Rafael, CA: New World Library, 1994.

———. *Quantum Healing.* New York: Bantam, 1989.

Cohen, Robert, and John Harop. *Creative Play Direction.* New Jersey: Prentice Hall, 1984.

Duncan, Isadora. *My Life.* New York: Liveright, 1927.

Easwaran, Eknath. *Gandhi the Man.* Petaluma, CA: Nilgiri Press, 1978.

Eisler, Riane. *The Chalice and the Blade.* San Francisco: Harper and Row, 1988.

Eliot, T. S. *Four Quartets, Collected Poems*, Harcourt Brace and Co. 1936.

Erikson, Erik. *Gandhi's Truth.* New York: W. W. Norton & Co., 1969.

Fadiman, James and Robert Frager. *Personality and Personal Growth.* New York: Harper and Row, 1976.

Ferrucci, Piero. *What We May Be.* Los Angeles: Jeremy Tarcher, 1982.

Frankl, Viktor. *The Will to Meaning.* New York: New American Library, 1969.

Fox, Matthew. *Creation Spirituality.* HarperSanFrancisco, 1991.

Gangaji. *You Are That.* Boulder, CO: Satsang Press, Vol 1., 1995, Vol 2., 1996.

For one who reads, there is no limit to the number of lives that may be lived.
LOUIS L'AMOUR

Gawain, Shakti. *Creative Visualization*. Mill Valley, CA:. Whatever Publishing, 1986.

Gendler, J. Ruth. *Book of Qualities*. New York: HarperCollins, 1988.

Gerber, Richard. *Vibrational Medicine*. Santa Fe, NM: Bear and Company, 1988.

Goleman, Daniel. *Emotional Intelligence*. New York: Bantam Books, 1995.

Good Housekeeping. "I've learned to look for the joy in each day." (Interview with Joan Lunden) April, 1997.

Gorbachev, Mikhail. *Perestroika*. New York: Harper and Row, 1987.

Gore, Al. *Earth in the Balance*. New York: Plume, 1993.

Grof, Stanislav and Christina Grof. *Spiritual Emergency*. Los Angeles: Jeremy Tarcher, 1989.

Grotowski, Jerzy. *Toward a Poor Theatre*. New York: Simon and Schuster, 1968.

Hagen, Uta with Haskel Frankel. *Respect for Acting*. New York: Macmillan Publishing Co., 1973.

Hanh, Thich Nhat. *Peace Is Every Step*. New York: Bantam, 1992.

Hardy, Jean. *A Psychology with a Soul*. New York: Routledge and Kegan Paul, 1987.

Houston, Jean. *The Possible Human*. Los Angeles: Jeremy Tarcher, 1982.

———. *The Search for the Beloved*. Los Angeles: Jeremy Tarcher, 1987.

Jung, Carl G. "The Meaning of Psychology for Modern Man." In Sir Herbert Read, et al., ed., *C. G. Jung: The Collected Works*. Vol 10. London: Routledge & Kegan Paul, 1964.

Kabat-Zinn, Jon. *Wherever You Go, There You Are*. New York: Hyperion, 1994.

Kaplan, Justin, ed. *Bartlett's Familiar Quotations*. Sixteenth edition. Boston: Little, Brown, and Co., 1992.

Kaslow, Amy. "A Garden Grows Jobs, Reaps Self-Esteem," *The Christian Science Monitor*. April 5, 1993.

Kidd, Sue Monk. *When the Heart Waits*. HarperSanFrancisco, 1991.

King, Janie. *The Ptaah Tapes*. Cairns, Australia: Triad Publishers, Ltd., 1991.

Kleefeld, Carolyn Mary. *Satan Sleeps with the Holy: Word Paintings*. Los Angeles: Horse and Bird Press, 1982. Distributed by Atoms Mirror Atoms, Inc., P. O. Box 221693, Carmel, CA 93922. (408) 626-2924.

Kramer, Sheldon. *Transforming the Inner and Outer Family*. New York: Haworth Press, 1995.

Lawlor, Anthony. *A Home for the Soul*. New York: Clarkson Potter, 1997.

Laskow, Leonard. *Healing with Love*. HarperSanFrancisco, 1992.

Maslow, Abraham. *Motivation and Personality*. New York: Harper and Row, 1970.

———. *Religion, Values, and Peak Experiences*. New York: Viking Press, 1971.

McLaughlin, Corinne and Gordon Davidson. *Spiritual Politics: Changing the World from the Inside Out*. New York: Ballantine Books, 1994.

Miller, Alice. *For Your Own Good*. New York: Farrar Straus Giroux, 1984.

Miller, Ronald. "Awakening the Spirit in Everyday Life: An interview with Sam Keen," *Science of Mind*. March 1996.

Mitchell, Edgar. "Outer Space to Inner Space," *Saturday Review*. Feb. 22, 1975.

Murphy, Michael, and Rhea White. *The Psychic Side of Sport*. Reading, MA: Addison-Wesley, 1978.

Narasimha Swami. *Self-Realization—The Life and Teachings of Sri Ramana Maharshi*. Tiruvannamalai: Sri Ramanasramam, 1976.

Newsweek, "The Young Master." April 28, 1997.

Pearce, Joseph Chilton. *Evolution's End*. HarperSanFrancisco, 1992.

Pearson, Carol. *Awakening the Heroes Within*. HarperSanFrancisco, 1991.

Perry, Whitall N. *A Treasury of Traditional Wisdom*. San Francisco: Harper and Row, 1986.

Prata, Kathleen. "The Resurgence of Earth-Based Religions: An interview with Wiccan Priestess Margot Adler," *Branches*. March/April, 1993.

Poonja, Sri H. W. L. *The Truth Is*. Yudishtara, 1995.

Prahbu, R. K., and R. U. Rao, eds. *The Mind of Mahatma Gandhi*. Ahmedabad: Navajihan, 1967.

Rigoglioso, Marguerite. "Awakening to the Goddess." *New Age Journal*, May/June, 1997.

Roth, Gabrielle. *Maps to Ecstasy*. San Rafael, CA: New World Library, 1989.

Rowan, John. *Subpersonalities: The People Inside Us*. New York: Routledge, 1990.

Rueffler, Margaret. *Our Inner Actors*. New York: Psychopolitical Peace Institute, 1995.

Siegel, Bernie. *Love, Medicine & Miracles*. New York: Harper and Row, 1986.

Sliker, Gretchen. *Multiple Mind*. Boulder, CO: Shambhala, 1992.

Stanislavski, Constantin. *Building A Character*. New York: Theater Arts Books, 1989.

———. *An Actor Prepares*. New York: Theater Arts Books, 1984.

———. *An Actor's Handbook*. New York: Theater Arts Books, 1963.

Staffort-Clark, E. *What Freud Really Said*. New York: Penguin Books, 1965.

We read books to find out who we are.
URSULA LeGUIN

Stone, Hal and Sidra Winkelman. *Embracing Our Selves*. Marina del Rey, CA: Devorss and Co., 1985.

Sweeney, Louise. "Young virtuoso in the old-fashioned fiery mold," *The Christian Science Monitor*. Nov. 10, 1987.

Taylor, Cathryn. *Inner Child Workbook*. Los Angeles: Jeremy Tarcher, 1991.

Thoreau, Henry David. *Walden and Other Writings of Henry David Thoreau*. New York: Modern Library, 1992.

van der Post, Laurens. *The Face Beside the Fire*. New York: William Morrow, 1953.

Vaughan, Stuart. *Directing Plays*. New York: Longman Publishing Group, 1993.

Weinraub, Bernard. "A Few Good Movies," *St Louis Post-Dispatch*. Dec 11, 1992.

Whitman, Walt. *Song of Myself*. Shambhala, 1993.

Williamson, Marianne. *A Return to Love*. New York: HarperCollins, 1992.

Yeomans, Anne. "Self Care During Dark Times," *Psychosynthesis in the Healing Professions* (eds. John Weiser and Thomas Yeomans). Toronto: Ontario Institute for Studies in Education, 1984.

Zohar, Danah. *The Quantum Self*. New York: William Morrow and Co., 1990.

Index

(Exercises are shown in **boldface** type.)